# HEALTH CHOICES

*Our Journey from Cancer's grasp*

## ...you should eat to avoid Heart Disease and Cancer.

*....with healthier food options*

*and cooking techniques.*

**By Michael and Vicki Bennett**

Published by:

## The Professional Image, Inc.

In the U.S: South Beach and South Florida

International: St. Croix, St. Thomas, Tortola, BVI

Contact us at: foodbrat@gmail.com

ISBN:   (Ebook)

(print) ISBN:  978-1513689470

Thanks to our Staff:

SENIOR Editor: Eileen Clark

ASSISTANT EDITOR: Vicki Bennett

Photographers: The Professional Image, Inc.

Copyright © 2021 by Michael Bennett ~ the FoodBrat ! All rights reserved.

No part of this publication may be reproduced, distributed, or transmitted in any form or by any means, including photocopying, recording, or other electronic or mechanical methods, without the prior written permission of the publisher, except in the case of brief quotations embodied in critical reviews and certain other non-commercial uses permitted by copyright law. For permission requests, write to the publisher, addressed "Attention: Permissions Coordinator," at the address below:

The Professional Image, Inc.

~South Florida~

96401 Overseas Hwy #3  |  Key Largo, Fl. 33037   |   305.799.8305

Ordering Information:

Quantity sales: Special discounts are available on quantity purchases by corporations, associations, and others. For details, contact the publisher at the address above.

Orders by U.S. trade bookstores and wholesalers. Please contact TPI

# Foreword:

*What to expect and Our Journey to get here...*

*Why do you want to read this book?*

- Every time you dine you are feeding to help or hinder a problem.
- We are going to help you make better decisions on what to eat.

*What are you going to find?*

- Healthier foods to eat that will help you in cases where a person is stricken with Heart disease or Cancer.

*How will this book help you?*

- Ideals of what healthy dining is and how to accomplish it.

*Who should read this book?*

- Anyone concerned with their health.
- Or someone looking to lose weight through a healthier diet.

*When can you start feeling better?*

- As soon as you change from your current dining habits you can feel better in days or a week.
- The longer you stay on this new routine the better you will feel about eating in general.

# The 1 - 2 - 3's of thinking about healthier eating:

### Look for Health Halo
...this means the packaging of a product and it's marketing promotes it's singularly healthy aspect, while it could be totally unhealthy in it's total (healthy) dining aspect.
- Like "organic" is featured on the label but you find out that it is hydrogenated ( that saturates the food) to thicken the product so it is more palatable.

### Train yourself to eat foods that take longer to chew.
- Healthier natural foods are less processed.

Unprocessed foods have more fiber and nutrient content which automatically makes this a better way of eating.

It has been proven that people eating a healthier diet live longer.

### Break old habits in eating.
- Don't binge drink sugary coffee because...you need to wake up. Sugar has been proven to energize **Cancer's** effects.

### Don't eat the sugary (yet touted) healthy food snacks thought to be more healthy, because they might be gluten free or organic.
- Giving into one good aspect of the food's quality and only looking at the aspects touted is a direct problem we need to deal with the rest of our lives.

# And....

- Commitment to being better has to be a goal and you have to tell others about your commitment. This makes you accountable for your own progress and become the expert that others might not see you.

- Always compare your results to you and not others that don't have your positive and negative yardstick. Positive results might not be small but the inclination to do more is based upon positive achieved goals or new healthy habits.

# *Our Journey started with our personal histories....*

My family has had its issues with health concerns. Most of my family has had Cancer and heart related health issues and some have died prematurely because of them.

I have become older than my father, because he died from heart problems when he was 44. When my wife was diagnosed with Cancer I would not let the doctor's opinions affect me the way it did with my father.

*Having Cancer or Heart problems are no longer death sentences. We are here to tell you it doesn't have to be for you either.*

*Growing up in a time with giant leaps in health-related knowledge is the way I can describe how I have chosen to look at my family's history as an educational function.*

Growing up in my family meant large portions of beef and high cholesterol foods at every meal. This is where I have broken with family traditions. My wife and I have been living relatively healthy for a few years but we have also taken a more relaxed vision of how to live. We live as we want on the beach on the American Caribbean. Eating healthy has just been a mission statement of living happier and healthier.

Since my family has been in the restaurant business since the *Great Depression*; my grandfather, my dad and uncle, wife, kids and all, it is natural for me to use our families talents in cooking food as a medicine for the body.

## I believe this has been true for my wife's recovery as well.

*Since the 1990's I have begun to feel generally better when I didn't eat pasta and breads. Come to find out I have been gluten intolerant for a very long time (ever since my oldest daughter decided she was going to be a vegetarian), I have stopped eating beef and for me it has produced great health results.*

*I had acute acid-reflux during most of my teenage life and into my twenties, only to find out it was just another family trait.*

My Great-Grandfather could not sleep lying down because the acid reflux wore out his throat and the contents in his stomach would come up and make him choke as he slept. After just one month I found that I didn't have any heart-burn related issues after I stopped the consumption of beef dishes. This first lead me to believe that eating well could mean better general health. After more than 25 years of not eating beef any longer, I experience no acid reflux conditions that plagued me in my earlier life.

*After my discovery in beneficial health effects from changing food related lifestyles, I started to teach others what I have found out in recipe experimentations.*

I have taught teens at school, other cooks and chefs and through my cookbooks hopefully I have reached out to help even more people.

I feel that if just a few people have found help from my words it makes it all worthwhile. I hope these ideas about food and my recipes help you in living a healthier life. But I really hope you tell others that you found this book's information helpful, and you continually tell others to spread my idea of a healthy way of life.

*Health is not about*

*Weight lost but,*

*The life you gain!*

# *Welcome to our journey*

*These things are just the start.*

*A healthy body is the result of many habits that support all dimensions of your life. It includes your mental well-being, your emotional health, your surroundings, and your spiritual life.*

Consuming enough fruits and vegetables as part of an overall healthy diet reduces the risk of many chronic diseases, including cardiovascular disease, type 2 diabetes, some cancers, and obesity.

2015–2020 Dietary Guidelines for Americans[1] recommend that adults should consume 1.5–2.0 cup equivalents of fruits and 2.0–3.0 cups of vegetables per day.

Although it may be hard to accept, the jury's still out on red meat. On eggs. On low carb versus low fat. On Paleo versus fully plant-based.

*QR code used to search for more information.*

---

1    https://health.gov/our-work/food-nutrition/previous-dietary-guidelines/2015

In fact, there's very little we can say with absolute certainty. Virtually everyone agrees, however:

- *Eat more minimally-processed whole foods.*
- *Eat fewer highly-processed food.*

- *More vegetables are better than fewer vegetables.*

- *Eating enough protein is crucial for health, performance, and body composition.*

## *Using this book:*

We need you to envision and see a picture I am trying to paint for you here.

What you can expect if you follow these details that follow is that you are going to feel better about eating and later you will feel better in general.

We are going to paint a picture for you that details how you too can relieve yourself from the pain of facing an early fight with Mother Nature.

★★★★★

### The beginning of this book is filled with the logic of healthy eating.

*Why some foods are better than others and I hope this information doesn't bog you down. It is here to prove that these recipes are made through proven scientific facts from various studies and fact gathering from around the world.*

I have set up the beginning of the book as an informational guide to what better healthy foods are and why they are healthier for you. I believe that our recipes are an assortment of healthy food related cure alls. Not every recipe has a purpose other than to be enjoyed .

*Every time you dine,*
*You are feeding or fighting a problem.*

These recipes, not all beautiful in picturesque glory but I feel each has a reason for you to try them. After years of cooking in restaurants I feel as though we all need to try different things in our lives. If we are lucky, we can find recipes that serve a dual purpose, to be healthy and tasty at the same time.

*Hippocrates said "let food be thy medicine, and let medicine by thy food."*

I believe this most of all. During my time as a chef, I have seen many chic food trends. Just like clothes fashion, what is in one day is out the next day. But we will be talking about proven food strategies. I have documented these ideals in the first portion of the book.

Medicine isn't always pretty and in most cases does not taste good but we are here to change that theory.

*We want you to create healthy habits, not a restrictive diet.*

Our medicine will mostly be *gluten-free* and almost all recipes are *vegetarian forward*. We start with basic food taken mostly only two steps removed from the earth in which it was grown. Food that is taken directly from the earth and not manipulated by human hands is better for you.

*Food direct from nature is right for you every time. Food touched by Man could never be as wise.*

We want recipes to be healthy and, yes as tasty as they are good looking. I have also have taken into consideration your time as well. I think most people caring for another person do not have the spare time to cook all day. So when you find a recipe in this book that you like and you can find it replicated at your local health foods store, buy it to save your time.

*Your best healthcare reforms start in your kitchen!*

Culinary short cuts don't work to live a better, healthy life. Yet everyone that is caring for someone needs a helping hand. I always say: if it is good and it works for you, then do it. Try buying in bulk and days ahead of cooking the recipe so you can cook at your own leisurely pace.

*Your time and health aren't valued as much As when they aren't here any longer.*

### **Hint:**

Always source out your best availability of quality food. The closer it comes from the earth the more time it usually takes to prepare dinner. This is a consideration you have to measure in your own circumstance. I always look for Organic foods first in the store. Price might be a consideration for you so always choose wisely.

Generally, you will find all seasonal products will be more available and of course the laws of supply and demand mean they will be cheaper. This is where canning and pickling comes into play like your grandmother knew.

*Paleo Diet is anything your Grandmother would recognize as food.*

Communication between the diner and the food preparer is of primary concern because they need to know why you are preparing food for dinner the way you are.

## *What do you want to accomplish at this point?*

*In your mind, list your concerns here so you can find corresponding parts of this book that highlight your needs.*

If we can address just a portion of your health concerns in this book we have succeeded in our goal to help others to live a better life.

For many of us reading this book it might be the first time we are admitting that we are looking for help from others. This is why we are here writing this book as well. I always tell everyone ask for help from others to help you in this quest. *We did!* The more we asked the more we found that we didn't ask enough. I assure you that the more you ask the more you will feel comfortable asking for more.

*This will grow into a theory and then become a strategy for future progress.* Ask yourself each time you jump to the next step in your strategy why is this important. When you find out why then, you have found your next progressive help question. Now think about this, what do you see as questions that you can ask doctors, friends and experts?

You will always find later, after an interview with experts, that there are more questions you forgot to ask. This is where telling people you need help, that their answers will help you formulate your next level of learning.

---

*We know that a minor calorie deficit and plant focused diet are going to optimize longevity.*

*When you study different popular diet regimens: plant based, Animal-based, **Paleo** and less on protein high content of fats related (**Keto**), low sugar, Vegan and so many others that have faded into the social structure of the American culture there will be one virtue that stands out....**diets** based in natural foods, proven in studies, are optimized for longevity of life.*

*There's no scientific evidence linking the carnivore diet with good health.[2]*

*We don't have data on what happens to people long-term. That includes no long-term data on weight and body composition, the digestive system, metabolic health, or anything else.*

- Due to a volume in high resistance weight training, people seeking longevity seek diets with less protein and high quality fats.

- Carbs, especially refined carbohydrates, have to be minimized and even completely eliminated.

- Longevity research has proven diets high in quality fats are composed of 70 % fats, 25 % protein and 5 % or less in Carbs are relative to longevity in life.

    Use QR codes to find out more information.

---

2    https://www.mcgill.ca/oss/article/health-nutrition/carnivore-diet-beefy-leap-faith

*Awareness that people truly don't understand these ideals is why we are writing this book.*

*...Several studies from Universities of Texas and Oklahoma have shown that good nutrition without good exercise produces poor results[3].*

You might truly know what you want but, are you aware that each set of these goals comes with a list of sacrifices?

## This is healthy eating....

Think of yourself as a raging river. The river is flowing between two banks - that hold the river in place and each side is molded by the river itself. When you veer from the center, the further you are from each (health-related) shoreline. The current that runs through the middle of it is the food you eat everyday.

- The center current would equate as *performance* food (*high carb-related* food). It is the food that delivers pure energy to you.

- The one side of the bank that holds this river in check we will call *Aesthetics (high-protein diets -- we all know the names of the diet)* and the other we will call *Longevity (foods related to the Mediterranean diet)*.

Use QR code to find out more information.

---

3   https://experiencelife.lifetime.life/article/how-exercise-affects-circulation-and-vice-versa/

The raging **waves** of the current in this river is your body circulating the energy derived from eating these foods. Your best bet is to be in the center of all the trends and get a little benefit from each diet trend. This is where you have to realize the further you go from one side of the river to the other, the larger the difference in results. Meaning, the further you go from the center to an edge of the river, the more drastic the foods you eat to change the results.

*Like a stream ... the further you get from one bank to the other, the awareness of what you are about to give up for the other, will become your restriction and benefit.*

Every desire you have for more information about this will become your quest. It has for us!

Every question and piece of information you uncover is a reason to be there. Focus on what is an appropriate date to enact your changes and then do them consistently over time.

Match your personal goals with your readiness, willingness and ability to carry them out. Especially in the context of other life demands such as work, school, family, traveling or whatever else you are dealing with in your life.

*The plan should be what is the most important to you.*

The second strategy is to create a balance of what you get from your results and the ability to consistently carry them out.

There will be trade-offs for progress. The daily ability to perform and complete the model for personnel changes are hard to accomplish but do-able.

- Don't overload with DETAILS you really don't need.

*My wife and I.*

# Table of Contents:
## Foreward:

How to Use this Book....... P. 5
The 1 - 2 - 3's about healthier eating...... P. 6
Our Journey away from Cancer's grasp ..... P.8-12
Using this Book..... P. 13
What do you want to accomplished at this point .... p. 17
This is healthy eating ...... p 19-21
Acknowledgments..... P. 25

### Chapter One: *Kaizen Cuisine ... p. 28*

We have written this book .... p. 29-31
How to start a better, Natural-diet, believe in this ... P. 33-35
Tips: for a Healthy Sustainable Diet .... P. 35-39
Guidelines and Simple Menu ideas ..... P. 39

### Chapter *One and a half*: Good for you Healthy Foods .....p. 42-46

Foods that GIVE you the opportunity to be your best ..... p. 47
Cancer looks like this. What does it feed on ..... P.49-50
Top Cancer-Fighting Foods ..... p. 51-70
Meat and our healthcare ..... p. 71
What is a Protein-Flip .... p. 74-76
Saturated Fats ..... P 76-79

### Chapter Two: Recipes ...... p. 80-188
Kaizen Foods ..... p. 82-89
Delectable delights, nibbles and such .... P. 91-142

### Chapter Three: Veggies and such..... p. 164-185

### Chapter Four: Sweet Stuff .... p.186

### Chapter Five: FYI .... p. 192-220

The best protein food substitute: Beans! .... P . 189-194
Lowering Your Cholesterol ..... p. 195-197
Seafood it can also provide wonderful benefits to your health..... p.. 197-200
Nut butters .... p. 201-202
Dietary fats and oils ..... p. 203-209
A list of common nutritional terms ..... p. 209-214
Background GF recipes .... p. 215-217
Probotics ..... p .217
Index ..... p. 222-225

# **<u>Acknowledgments:</u>**

*This book has been written from research directly retrieved from the Internet.*

*I have used terms, definitions and theories from experts based around the globe to inform you of all this information.*

Following the results you find on *healing yourself through the food you eat* is something you have to tell others about. The more times you tell your story, the more you see all the little gains that you have accomplished add up to a healthy success.

*Symptoms are not bad vibes, they are messengers that you need to be healthier.*

Always compare the results that you have accomplished to a life without trying to make a difference. Because the more you work towards a goal, the more you see the results in a positive nature.

Achieving small goals is always the best way to continue on a healthy gradient. I have given you my experiences here in this book so you will avoid the potholes we fell into. Hopefully you will find our advice helps you on your journey towards a new healthy lifestyle.

*One's health is never cherished as much as when symptoms appear.*

# Chapter One:

## "Kaizen Cuisine"

**Improving your health through the food you eat!**

*"Kaizen" is an Asian term meaning*

*"Continuous improvement"*

*My wife and I wanted to tell you what we have done to fight Cancer through the foods we ate....*

# Although you won't feel like eating, you have to.

*All the foods in this book will help you stay strong.*

*I am going to warn you when there are concerns in proposed food choices that could affect other aspects of your health.*

*When you have Cancer the most important treatment you will need to do is feed your body to help heal yourself.*

**We have written this book in a way that tells you what has worked for us in our quest for a healthier life including heart-healthy choices.**

The disease won't make it easy for you. When you go through treatments ...you have to force yourself to eat right and in the end food *I think* will make everything else you do seem easier.

You have to remember everything you do now is different. Being different is change. Change is sometimes the hardest to do but when you think about it....doing these different things changes the things that got you here in the first place.

*Your body needs energy to produce the results you need….*

*energy to fight and win.*

You don't have to change everything but the more you change the easier it is to find out what you need to do differently in your life.

Here are a few **simple changes** that make the rest of your tasks easier…. Start by eating more ….

- Lean protein foods (seafood is my number one go to),
    - Fin fish are the best in this category, shellfish species have cholesterol concerns.
- Eggs, if you don't have heart concerns,
    - Egg substitutes have better results for those who have heart-healthy concerns. I like to add Tofu into cuisine as a health alternative.
- Milk products; all types (I love Yogurt for dessert),
- Cheese, (when heart concerns aren't an issue),
    - I love this food category because there are so many taste variances for your dining option. *When you look at cheeses from around the world, there are cultures that base their entire daily food emphasis upon cheeses….*

- - There are Goat's milk cheeses, Sheep's milk cheese (both are good for heart health related concerns). You are not limited to Cow's milk cheeses.

- Beans, my favorite healthy **protein substitute**.

  - I can't emphasize how good all of these foods are for you. Any dry bean (white, black, red, etc…) combined with any rice is a complete protein meaning you can live a healthful life…. just eating these two items,,,,, for your entire lifespan.

- Nuts and Seeds; especially in my salads,

  - Many nut butters (and Milk-Almond) are just coming out into the marketplace. Trial and error is how we have discovered what we like.

- Colorful veggies, anything bright you can see on the produce shelves that looks tasty are probably a great choice.

  - Most common choices in veggies is the closer to the earth in which they are from the better they are for you. Meaning: the common thought of food was better when mom cooked all day (because she had to do everything from scratch) has and will always be better for you.

  - In general any veggie that is bright has greater amounts of vitamins. Vitamin C is higher in ripe bell peppers than an orange.

  - Carrots are great for the eyes and the bulk in fiber will keep you full for hours.

- And for dessert and healthy snacking: Fruits:
    - I love the bright-colored berries (high in antioxidants), apples and new favorite healthy snacks including Sour Sop known to be 50 percent better than any other fruit source for it's Cancer fighting abilities. Besides being food that will keep you healthy, most are very filling. Try eating 2 cups a day. You will find yourself less hungry for foods that made it easy for you to put on body weight.

*Eat lots of protein and healthy calories....this will keep your body strong and help repair damage from your Cancer treatment.*

## How to start a better, *natural diet*.

*Get and Stay Motivated:*

Here we will define and explain the term "motivation" ….this has always been my weakness.

- **"*I need this motivation to become a habit.*"**
    - And this will lead to doing the same things for the same reason everyday which makes me feel "normal".

### Setting Goals:

Define your goals like: what keeps you motivated. Say them out loud to yourself. List the examples of your goals and then repeat them often.

## *Benefits and Costs of Losing Weight.*

### *Following my cooking tips you will find that your body will lose weight.*

# Believe in What You Are Doing…..

*….using your self-help speech about the accomplishments you have done and what you plan to do. You will see for yourself the satisfaction you get from these accomplishments and the relation to weight loss will help you continue on with this new lifestyle plan.*

### **Fats:**

Do your research into fats to avoid them, essential fatty acids, cooking with fats. Follow the guidelines found in this book and you will see results in your total health.

### **Salt:**

Salt (sodium *chloride*) is bad in excess. It may only be partially true. Salt is important in the body for several functions. *Use in limited doses.*

### **Sweeteners:**

Sweeteners are an energy sources that help **Cancer** to grow in your body. Limit your consumption of sugar, corn syrup, etc.… and insert safe artificial sweeteners like: Stevia, Truvia and Erythritol.

### **Cookery History:**

There are many food trends including Paleo (a Prehistoric cooking/ food harvesting/preparation ideology) that has worked for people. The closer to the Earth that you get your food, **I believe**, will always be better for you. Also, the side effects of foods that are naturally healthier because they are "Natural", yet carry risks of Cholesterol. (beef, butter, etc…)

*Non-Modified foods -- used in getting back to basics, are meant to be a guide on how to live a healthier life. You have to decide if the side effects are tolerable with your own health conditions.*

# **_Tips_**
## *for a Healthy Sustainable Diet:*

I live in a state that is notorious for its high food prices, so I'm all too aware just how costly it is to eat well on the cheap, but some of my tactics may work for you:

Stop buying food products and start buying real food. Crackers (as much as we love them), boxed cereal, and packaged granola bars are a food product, even if they're organic – and they're expensive. Swapping to organic cereal may eliminate some contaminants from your diet, but it's still not real food. Instead, try homemade breakfast alternatives like granola, oatmeal or muffins. Snack on baby carrots, apples, nuts and seeds.

Shop the bulk food aisle. The bulk food aisle at my health food offers primarily organic versions of dry beans, pasta, nuts and seeds. Sold by the pound, these items are generally less expensive than their packaged counterparts, saving you money and creating less waste.

Buy in season. Fruits and vegetables are less expensive when they're in season in your region. Indulge like crazy when strawberries are in season and then let it go. Buying strawberries from South America is expensive and terrible for our environment, not to mention not sustainable at all.

*Visit farmers' markets.* If your community has more than one, check them all out. I find that some cater to a higher end crowd, and thus have higher prices. Find the market that has the best prices and frequent that one.

*Make friends with a gardener.* Successful gardeners generally have an abundance to share. Offer to help in the garden or barter a skill you have in exchange for surplus vegetables.

*Grow some of your own food.* If you're new to gardening, there is an initial investment in getting set up as you work to either amend soil or fill pots with potting mix, but in the long run it will save money. Let's say you spend $5 on a bag of potting soil and salvage a pot or bucket to use for planting. Spend $2 on a packet of lettuce seeds, sow them, and in a month's time you'll be rewarded with multiple heads of lettuce.

*Cook double.* Instead of making one lasagna, make two and freeze one for another night. Make twice as many pizza doughs as you'll need and freeze the excess. Frozen meals will save you on busy nights, eliminating the what's-for-dinner panic and preventing an unexpected expense for take-out. This not only saves time and money, but it saves energy as well.

*Eat less meat.* Unless you raise your own or have access to an inexpensive meat source, buying meat is expensive. Buying sustainable meat is even more expensive. If you're a meat loving household, Meatless Monday is a good inspiration and offers up a variety of meatless recipes.

*Learn to love beans.* They're filling and cheap. Homemade chili and stewed beans are an inexpensive meal option.

*Stop snacking.* We are a nation of Snackers, but it's an expensive habit.

### *Get started eating natural...*

Looking for a healthy eating plan that consists of natural foods to improve your appearance and health should be a top priority. Through the course of this article I will reveal to you a healthy eating plan that will promote safe natural weight loss, improve your overall health and is easy to follow.

Unfortunately, to many people are eating more than their share of fast food. Many people eat fast food on a daily basis and never give any thought of the harm they do their body. This is probably because they grew up on fast foods so it never occurs to them how unhealthy these foods are. Well, that is until they start having health problems and their doctor informs them the food they are eating is slowly killing them. Does this sound like you?

It is not only foods from fast food restaurants but many of the meals people prepare at home from processed foods that are filled with preservatives. Everyone should realize that many of the preservatives you find in processed foods are unhealthy. Over a period of time eating processed foods may lead to diabetes, heart disease or colon cancer.

It is no shock that *1 out of every 3 Americans are obese*. To make things worse when many people decide to follow a diet they end up following some trendy fad diet that claims instant weight loss but is not a well-balanced diet utilizing the major foods groups. Too many times I witness an individual opt for a diet that promises that you will lose 10 pounds immediately. What they don't tell you is most of the people gain that weight right back and even a few pounds more. Guess what, starvation diets are neither healthy nor successful diets.

When you select a ***healthy diet plan*** to follow you need to consider these things. The healthy diet plan you select should contain foods from all the major food groups. The human body needs a balanced amount of proteins, carbohydrates and fats. In most cases you will need to prepare your meals by using natural and organic foods. Today many supermarkets provide a section that contains these healthy foods.

Stop eating foods from fast food restaurants. I know they are convenient, quick and many times offer dollar menus to persuade you to purchase but these are the foods you need to fully avoid.

One healthy diet plan you need to be familiar with is the Paleo diet. This simple diet plan utilizes natural foods similar to what the caveman may have eaten over 10,000 years ago.

# Guidelines and simple menu ideas

*The resetting of your diet can be as simple or as gourmet as you wish. For simplicity, it can be as easy as a shake, salad, and a stir-fry. Here are some ideas to get you started:*

### *Salad Substitution options:*

- You can use any other greens instead of lettuce[4]. Look at the Internet. There are so many choices for you to try; you might be overwhelmed. Try to change your choices to give yourself a varied taste palette.

- Try any type of beans. Chick-peas and navy beans are great options. I love this idea for adding "*High-in-Protein*" foods to your diet to replace beef. Also adding chicken, seafood or tempeh can be used in place of America's favorite protein (*beef*).

- Other oils can be used instead of olive oil. Nut oils have similar effects of Olive oil but the flavors can be boldly different. Most nut oils are good for you.

- Other seasoning blends can replace Mrs. Dash.

---

4   https://www.gardeningknowhow.com/edible/vegetables/greens/lettuce-substitutes.htm#:~:text=A%20common%20alternative%20to%20lettuce,and%20it%20contains%20more%20nutrients.&text=This%20robust%20perennial%20will%20give,bitterness%20if%20not%20prepped%20properly.

**Stir Fry Substitution options:**

- There are unlimited vegetable choices these days. Explore your options.

- Try lean food substitutions including: tofu, fin-fish (Mahi Mahi), pork or tempeh.

- Other oils can replace toasted sesame seed oil.

- Other seasonings to replace soy sauce like coconut Aminos.

  - Although to use soy is avoidable, a natural soy sauce is fermented instead of chemically altered like commercial varieties and are fine for your health in normal quantities.

    - Coconut vinegar, Fish sauce (from premium companies in Asia), Ume plum vinegar is a great substitute.

    - *I use* **fish sauce** *as a seasoning to replace salt I would have used in recipes that extend beyond just stir-fries.*

# Chapter One~

## *and a half*:

## Good for you Healthy Foods

*Not to say all these foods have to be included in you daily diet; I am saying if you have a choice, when you add these foods into your life, you will notice a difference.*

*Do you see that the portion sizes are different from what you are used to? This is one way we are going to elevate your new healthy lifestyle.*

## *These are foods that I have found to work for us.*

*…. go in a logical order, each one building on the next.*

*…. they have to have a specific purpose.*

*…little actions add up to big results.*

....Everything you learn from a new cooking style is just data and information.

- ....if your results are going the way you expect, great!

- This data gives you clues about where you might need to make changes, based upon how you feel.

> *<u>**Next**</u> and most importantly are process indicators ~*
>
> *in other words ~ How are your body and mind feeling*
>
> *or doing along this journey.*

## *Learning from your results*
## *are an iterative process.*

- Every decision should be based on data and then it is an assessment of good or bad results *questioning*, why they didn't turn out like you expected, rather than on guessing or imagining something unseen is the major changeable fact.

- You should always be asking yourself:......Is this working for my needs?

- How do I know for sure whether it's working? Has enough time passed to get accurate results to measure.

- What does my results say I should be doing next?

    - ....this is outcome-based decision making. And it takes time and dedication to the effort believing you chose the right direction to travel.

## Ask Yourself...

- How well are you sleeping?

- What is your mood every day?

- How much energy do you have?

- How hungry are you every day?

.....the recording process data and indicators gives you a kind of "running news feed".

> ***So, by focusing on behaviors that matter,***

.....you should be tracking how consistent you are with new behaviors.

.....you should get a baseline. What is normal and how does it feel...do you need to push for more? Or do feel like you are doing enough.

## *There are three important reasons why we look for what's already working well.*

- **First,** looking at where you are already succeeding, or moving towards your goals, this leads us to clues about our next actions.

  - Often, it's just a matter of keeping a fettered dieter going in the right direction, or giving a little boost to keep that existing momentum up.

- **Second,** calling out what you are already doing well is very motivating.

  - So the more you can focus on replicating the good things you are already doing is better.

- Find the right level of difficulty that you are ready, willing, and able to do.

- Give yourself one task at a time.

- Focus on making sure you can be *consistent* with that task.

- Monitor what happens…while making sure you have realistic expectations based on their nutritional level and how fast you are ready, willing, and able to go.

- Look especially for how consistently you are achieving key behaviors.

    - Then adjust, focusing mostly on what's going well and trying to do more of that.

### Positive progress focus

*Comparing yourself to some superhero ideal doesn't work. It makes you feel inadequate. Like you'll never get there.*

- Which is why it's important to seek out—and shine a light on—any and all positive progress.

*My Wife Vicki*

# *Foods that GIVE you the opportunity to be your best...*

### Healthy Proteins – Serving Sizes - Once a day:

Black cod / sablefish – 3 ounces

Chicken breast - 3 ounces

Cod – 3 ounces

Protein Powder, Vegetable based– 1 scoop

Sardines – 3 ounces (or Mackerel)

Turkey breast - 3 ounces

Turkey, Lean ground - 3 ounces

Wild Alaskan salmon - 3 ounces

### Several times per week or less:

Turkey bacon – 3 pieces

Oysters – 3 ounces

Canadian bacon – 3 pieces

Coconut yogurt, Nonfat unsweetened – 1 cup

Ham, lean– 3 ounces

Lamb – 3 ounces

Pork chop – 3 ounces

Pork loin, lean – 3 ounces

Rainbow trout – 3 ounce

# Fighting through Food:

### <u>Here is a list of the limited foods...</u>

- **Deep-fried**, grilled, barbecued, baked meats since subjecting animal protein to high heat creates **carcinogenic** byproducts called hetero cyclic amines.

- Excessive intake of salt, sugar, and oily (fried) foods.

- Red meat and *processed* meats; such as bacon, ham, sausages and deli-style cold cuts.

## *Here are things we have found that helped us be proactive in fighting Cancer.*

*You might be wondering why we are starting out the book in this way. It is because we feel that these food elements have helped tremendously in our search for healthier food options.*

# *Cancer looks like this...*

There are many Cancer-related illnesses that won't be discussed in this book because there are just too many. We are going to talk about what has worked for us and it is limited to *our* details in fighting my wife's Cancer.

- Our story started when my wife (almost 60 years of age) went to the ER because she was having chest pain, similar to previous heart related problems stemming from AFIB. Since we have changed her eating habits months ago, it has been more than twelve months now without a recurrence.

    - *I believe that her AFIB was resolved by the change in diet and regular exercises she does almost every day.*

    - *A diet heavy in fresh seafood is our main nutritional adjustment.*

  - Everyone is different but if your breast Cancer tumor is smaller than the approximate size of a small nut (2 cm) it is considered to be a **stage 0**, **it is very treatable and survivable**. My wife's Cancerous tumor was smaller than half a centimeter.

    - *Not all Cancers are curable but my wife's life was saved because of early detection.* **<u>Everyone should remember that!</u>**

# **What does Cancer feed on?**

- Every cell in your body uses blood sugar (glucose) for energy.

    - *Cancer cells use about 200 times more than normal cells.*

- Tumors that start in the thin, flat (squamous) cells in your lungs (...*like my Wife's Cancer*) gobble up even more glucose. *They need huge amounts of sugar to fuel their growth.*

    - This is why we are eating differently. The foods that are related to a Keto Diet will help you format a new way of eating healthier.

        - Researchers have found that sugar-sweetened sodas contain large quantities of *sucrose* and fructose, which give them the highest glycemic load compared to other foods or beverages. These higher concentrations of glucose and insulin may lead to conditions that have been associated with higher risk of breast cancer.

# **Top Cancer-Fighting Foods:**

Why is Flaxseed[5] good for you?

These tiny seeds are packed with **omega-3** fatty acid ALA, Lignans and Fiber, all of which have been shown to have many potential health benefits.

- They can be used to *improve* digestive health, lower blood pressure and bad *cholesterol*.

  - Research has found that they can reduce the risk of cancer and may benefit people with diabetes.

Should you eat Flax seeds raw? **No!**

- **Flax** seeds are safe for most people when consumed in moderate amounts. But there are some things to keep in mind before you take flax seeds to lose weight. **Don't consume raw or unripe flax seeds**. Not only will they cause indigestion, they may also contain toxic compounds.

Do Flaxseed contain estrogen to help women?

- **Flaxseed** is the richest dietary source of **Lignans**, a type of phyto-estrogen.

  - A phyto-estrogen is a plant nutrient that is somewhat similar to the female **hormone** estrogen.

  - Due to this similarity, Lignans may have **estrogenic** and/or anti-estrogenic effects in the body.

---

5   https://www.healthline.com/nutrition/benefits-of-flaxseeds

- **Estrogen**-progestin therapy...Although **estrogen** alone improves the symptoms of menopause .... It also can increase the risk of cancer of the uterus (Endometrial Cancer).

  ....Studies have shown that adding a progestin to the estrogen lowers[6] the risk of endometrial cancer back to normal.

- Does hormone therapy kill cancer cells?

  - **Hormones** are chemicals made by glands, such as the ovaries and testicles.

  - **Hormones** help some types of cancer cells grow, such as breast cancer and prostate cancer.

  .....In other studies and cases, hormones **can** kill cancer cells or make cancer cells grow less.

## *How can you add Flax Seeds to your daily meals?*

- You can *grind* Flax Seeds

  - Sprinkle them on warm oatmeal or cold breakfast cereal.

  - Use it in your pancake batter.

  - You can add a teaspoon of ground flaxseed to sandwich spreads; mayonnaise, dressings or spicy mustard spreads.

---

6   https://www.theatlantic.com/health/archive/2012/01/how-progestin-a-synthetic-female-hormone-could-affect-the-brain/251299/

- Make your yogurt snack - protein packed - by mixing a tablespoon of ground flaxseed into each 8-ounce portion of yogurt.
- If you are in need of sweet treats, bake ground flaxseed into cookies, muffins, breads and other baked goods.

**Can you eat Flaxseed every day?**

- Research has found that consuming flaxseed daily may also help your cholesterol levels.
  - *Studies have shown that Flaxseed can lower the level of **LDL** or "**bad**" cholesterol in your vinous system…. that has been linked to an increased risk of heart disease, obesity and diabetes.*

Does flaxseed make your breasts bigger?

- *They might be the last natural method to grow your breasts!*
  - *These seeds have been known to increase breast tissue growth and can help your breasts grow larger.*

## Is it OK to eat Chia seeds and Flax seeds together?

Both **Flax** and **Chia seeds** are great additions to a healthy diet and those especially worried about getting too much omega 6 …. like those people who have adapted their lives to a Paleo diet.

…. Add both of these seeds to help balance the Omega 6 to Omega 3 ratio in your diet.

## Are Chia or Flax seeds healthier?

*They have several of the same benefits. Chia seeds can be as much help to your health as the more well-known 'super seed' flax, but unlike flax seed, you don't need to grind them to reap the health benefits.*

*However, please note that those who suffer from certain nut or seed-based allergies may be allergic to chia seeds. Those on blood thinning or blood pressure medication should also get in touch with a medical professional before including chia seeds in their regular diet.*

|          | Flax Seeds: | Chia Seeds: |
|----------|-------------|-------------|
| Calories | 150         | 137         |
| Carbs    | 8 grams     | 12 grams    |
| Fiber    | 8 grams     | 11 grams    |
| Protein  | 5 grams     | 4 grams     |
| Fat      | 12 grams    | 9 grams     |
| Omega-3  | 6400 mg     | 4900 mg     |
| Omega-6  | 1700 mg     | 1600 mg     |

- **Flax seeds** also contain significantly more manganese, copper and potassium than Chia seeds. This is good news for women and men….
    - For Women….**Chia seeds** contain slightly fewer calories and more fiber than Flax seeds…..**Chia seeds** contain 18% of **daily** recommended intake of calcium.
        - Flax seeds are distinctively better for *women* because they contain **1.5–2 times** more of the bone-strengthening minerals *calcium* and *phosphorus*, as well as slightly more iron.

- ***Chia seeds**....are a great source of fiber, omega fatty acids, protein and antioxidants.*
  - Chia seeds also provide our bodies with healthy fats like *omega-3* and *omega-6* fatty acids.
- **Use them...**
  - As a thickener....dry **Chia seeds** swell up and absorb about 10–12 times their weight when mixed into a liquid. Great for making shakes.
    - *As the seeds absorb liquids. Everything they are added to gets thicker, or creamier AND more fulfilling.*
  - They will make you feel fuller for longer periods between eating. Its fiber helps slow digestion and makes you feel fuller by soaking up fluid and expanding in your digestive tract.
    - Chia seeds are rich in fiber. Thus consuming chia seeds water in the morning can give a boost to your digestion and improve bowel movement.

*The chia seeds are a 'super' food because they deliver the maximum amount of nutrients with minimum calories.*

## *Two-Tablespoons of Chia seeds contain and boasts*:

They have 64% *more* potassium than bananas (and fewer calories of course);

- **Twice** the antioxidants of blueberries;
- It boasts 41% of your daily required fiber content;
- They have **5 times** as much Calcium as milk;
- They have **100% more** Omega-3 than salmon;
- They have **3 times** as much Iron as spinach;
- They have 20% of your daily need of protein and 30% of your need in magnesium.

- *As a source of **omega-3** fatty acids, chia seeds can help reduce inflammation and decrease the chance of developing deep vein and arterial thrombosis (an issue for me as well) or arrhythmia.*
    - Studies have found that **Chia seeds** can also help *raise* HDL, the healthy cholesterol, which will help reduce plaque in your arteries, improve brain and cognitive function.
        - One way amino acids improve health is by promoting the production of neurotransmitters. **Tryptophan,** an amino acid in chia seeds, can help people feel more calm and sedated.
        - Chia seeds also help the brain increase production and reception of **serotonin** -- the "happy hormone" -- and regulate melatonin levels that helps you relax and sleep well.

- Chia seeds have been found to be *high* in **antioxidants**.
    - **Antioxidants** prevent your body from reproduction of free radicals and reduce their ratio to healthy cells.
        - Unchecked, free radicals in your body naturally, can contribute to premature aging and cancerous growths.
            - Coffee is a rich source of disease-fighting antioxidants[7]. And studies have shown that it may reduce cavities, boost athletic performance, improve moods, and stop headaches -- not to mention reduce the risk of type 2 diabetes, colon cancer, liver cancer, gall stones, cirrhosis of the liver, and Parkinson's diseases

*Do Chia seed help keep you balanced on the Keto-diet?*

- *With 31 grams of fat and 17 grams of protein per 100 grams (you usually only eat a fraction of that amount), chia seeds are **keto-diet friendly** and make an excellent ingredient for many low-carb recipes.*
    - Although nuts and seeds do contain sugar and carbs, chia seeds contain carbs which are actually fiber, which does not increase blood sugar or jeopardize ketosis.

*However, please note that those who suffer from certain nut or seed-based allergies may be allergic to chia seeds. Those on **blood thinning or blood pressure medication** should also get in touch with a medical professional before including chia seeds in their regular diet.*

---

[7] https://www.webmd.com/diet/features/the-buzz-on-coffee#1

*These are the Foods we have added to our meals ...to make our fight successful.*

- **Apples** contain polyphenols that have promising *anticancer* properties.
    - *Polyphenols are plant-based compounds that may prevent inflammation, cardiovascular disease, and infections.*
    - *Some research suggests that polyphenols possess anticancer and tumor-fighting properties.*
- **Cruciferous vegetables** contain beneficial nutrients, including vitamin C, vitamin K, and manganese. *Cruciferous* vegetables are **broccoli, cauliflower and kale**. Cruciferous vegetables also contain **sulforaphane**, a plant compound with *anticancer* properties.

*One study shows that sulforaphane significantly inhibits cancer cell growth and stimulates cell death in colon cancer cells[8].*

---

8     https://cancerres.aacrjournals.org/content/60/5/1426.short

*Another study shows that sulforaphane in combination with genistein, a compound in soybeans, can significantly **inhibit** breast cancer tumor development and size. Sulforaphane also inhibits histone deacetylase, an enzyme with links to cancer development.*

- **Cruciferous Vegetables**. …

    o These are the vegetables, also called Brassica vegetables, whose four-petal flowers form the shape of a cross – **cruciferous** means "cross-bearing." Cruciferous vegetables include: *Swiss chard, broccoli, cabbage, brussel sprouts, cauliflower, watercress, radish, rapini, arugula, spinach, turnip, kale, and bok choy*.

        - Spinach and other green leafy vegetables — Spinach is a **powerhouse** of nutrients whether eating raw, juiced or lightly cooked.

- The **Cancer-*fighting*** properties are attributed to compounds called glucosinolates[9], which are found in **all** cruciferous vegetables. Upon ingestion, glucosinolates break down to isothiocyanates and indoles, which are *associated* with **decreased** inflammation, lowering the risk of cancer.

    o The current study suggests that **cruciferous vegetable** intake is associated with **reduced breast cancer** risk, in particular with broccoli and cauliflower intakes. The inverse association of cruciferous vegetable consumption with *breast cancer* risk seems to be more apparent in premenopausal women.

---

9    https://www.verywellfit.com/what-are-glucosinolates-and-why-are-they-good-for-me-2505908

- What is the *healthiest* cruciferous vegetable?
    - **Brussels sprouts** have the most vitamin E (about 9% of the Daily Value) and vitamin B-1 (15% Daily Value).
        - **Broccoli** and **Brussels sprouts** again have the most healthy plant omega-3s: A cup of broccoli contributes about 200 milligrams, and a cup of Brussels sprouts about 260 milligrams.
    - Are cruciferous vegetables better raw or cooked? ...if they are **cooked** vs. eating them **raw**.
        - *Cooking* cruciferous vegetables such as broccoli, cauliflower, and cabbage helps them release *indole*, an organic compound *that can* fight off pre-cancerous cells. ... Cooking makes it *easier for the fiber and their nutrients to move* through your system.
    - Do Broccoli sprouts fight cancer?
        - Studies done in the lab and in animals show that broccoli sprouts contain **Sulforaphane**[10]....... which has *anticancer properties*. In a study conducted in humans, broccoli sprouts were found to play a role in eliminating toxic pollutants.
            - *Ideally:* **Sulforaphane**, *is one of the primary phytochemicals in broccoli and other cruciferous vegetables that helps them* **prevent** *cancer.* It has been shown in the latest studies to selectively target and **kill cancer** cells while leaving normal Prostate cells healthy.

---
10    https://www.sciencedirect.com/topics/biochemistry-genetics-and-molecular-biology/sulforaphane

- **Folate-Rich Foods**. This B-complex vitamin can be found in many "good for you" foods. ... Research has shown that **eating** fruits and vegetables rich in **folate** is associated with a reduced risk of certain types of *Cancer*.

    - Specifically, **folate** and **folic acid** have been linked with potential reductions in the risk of breast, colon, rectal, and pancreatic cancers[11].

        - **Leafy Green Vegetables**. The word folate actually derives from foliage, which refers to the leafy green veggies that contain some of the highest natural concentrations of the vitamin found in any food.

- **Graviola** (**Annona muricata**); known commonly in the Caribbean and the Americas as **Soursop** (or **Guanabana**) …. is a fruit tree that grows in tropical rain forests. Other fruits in the same family of (*mostly growing in South American and Asian countries*) Annonaceae would also be; **Atemoya** (or SweetSop), **Cherimoya** (or Custard Apple), Bullocks heart, PawPaw (native to the southeastern US) and **Rollinia** *delicios*.

*Graviola leaf extract studies have shown it to stop the growth cycle of lung cancer cells.*

---

11     https://www.ncbi.nlm.nih.gov/pmc/articles/PMC1856406/

*Because many of these fruits are newly discovered by Americans, researchers are just now looking at them. This family of fruit is rich in fiber, vitamins, minerals and uniquely may boost immunity, fight inflammation, and promote eye and heart health.*

- **Cherimoya** is loaded with free-radical fighting antioxidants. Also packed with high levels of nutrients to fight off oxidative stress (*which* ***Cantaloupe*** *also provides*) … where studies have found positive associations with chronic illnesses, including cancer and heart disease.
    - ***Cherimoya*** also elevates B-6. It helps create neurotransmitters like: serotonin and dopamine, which help elevate a good mood and may fight *depression* in most people.
    - ***Catechin***: a *flavonoid* in this fruit has been observed to ***stop*** up to *100% of breast Cancer cell growth in a test-tube study.*
  - You can use this fruit, roots, seeds, and leaves to treat all kinds of ailments, including Cancer. Modern scientists have been studying the plant for close to 50 years. They see potential promise in ***Graviola***.
    - *Hint: To use, remove the fruit's pulp from the skin and seeds. Experimental studies of random people in these areas associate high amounts of consumed Annona fruits to an increased risk of a specific type of Parkinson's disease.*
  - **Vitamin D**. This fat-soluble vitamin which helps absorb calcium to build strong teeth and bones may also build protection against Cancer.

- The researchers also found that among women where **vitamin D** blood levels are an evaluator... the higher their level, the *lower* their risk of **breast cancer**.
  - But the study *did not prove* that higher vitamin D levels prevent breast cancer, just that there was an association.

- **Tea**. ...Green Tea has been recommended more than any other study.
  - Most reports on Teas are *inconclusive*.
    - Ginger root tea is still being reviewed to this day. In Asia, ginger plays an important role in every meal.

- Cooked **Lentils**. ...

  *Eating lentils daily can include these health benefits: besides filling your tummy up to help with weight loss by eating this fiber-packed, healthy legume.*

  - Lentils are a good **alternative protein** source that your body demands and eating them decreases your hunger because of their high level of soluble fiber....
    - They can also lower Cholesterol which improves your heart health.
    - Great Northern Beans are associated with the same effects.

- **Elderberry** Health Benefits
    - *The berries and flowers of elderberry are packed with antioxidants and vitamins that may boost your immune system. They could help tame inflammation, lessen stress, and help protect your heart.*

*Elderberry has been known to man since the prehistoric period, according to scientists, and elderberry recipes were widely used as natural remedies in ancient Egypt.*

The Romans used elderberry juice as hair dye, and the wood of the elderberry tree was used to make combs, dolls, pegs for shoemakers, needles for weaving musical instruments, and skewers for butchers. This plant was used by Native Americans as a natural medicine, body polish, dye, jewelry and musical instruments, hunting whistles, and much more.

DURING THE 1995 PANAMA FLU OUTBREAK, THE GOVERNMENT USED IT AS A NATURAL MEANS TO COMBAT THE FLU, AND IT SERVED TO DECREASE THE INCIDENCE OF THE FLU: THEREBY HELP TO END THE EPIDEMIC.

Elderberry is a herb that is native to Africa, Europe, and areas of Asia. Sambucus is a flowering plant genus in the Adoxaceae family, and its berries and flowers are effective natural medicines. The plant has deciduous leaves, white flowers (elderflower), and berries that ripen from green to red to black.

Elderberry is also rich in flavonoid, which are strong antioxidants that protect cells from injury, and anthocyanidins, which are chemical compounds that are immunostimulant properties.

Elderberries are high in iron and potassium, as well as vitamins A, C, and B6. The raw berries are comprised of roughly 80% sugar, 18% carbohydrates, and less than 1% protein and fat.

It is protective against infections such as influenza, herpes, viral infections, and bacterial infections. Elderberry can be used as a natural treatment for influenza A and B, according to a report published in the Journal of Traditional and Complementary Medicine.

This is due to its effectiveness against all strains of influenza virus studied, clinical outcomes, low cost, and lack of side effects. Many aspects of the elderberry can be used — the flowers, bark, stems, and leaves are frequently used for their excellent health benefits."

*This awesome plant contains more flavonoid than blueberries, cranberries, goji berries, and blackberries, and it has the following health benefits:*

Elderberries improve the immune system due to the inclusion of anthocyanidins, which are chemical compounds with strong immunostimulant properties. Elderberry extract is one of the most effective and best therapies for cold and flu symptoms.

For decades, the berry and flower have been used to treat diabetes. Elderflower extract has been shown to promote glucose synthesis and insulin release, lowering blood sugar levels.

The flowers of the elder plant are an important herbal allergy treatment because they improve the immune system and soothe inflammation. It cleanses the liver and removes toxins, and herbalists say it can treat hay fever-like symptoms.

Elderberry is often used in beauty products because it contains antioxidants, vitamin A, and bioflavonoids, which enhance the appearance of the skin, avoid premature aging, and provide a healthy skin glow.

- **Cantaloupe....**

    *is loaded with free-radical fighting antioxidants. Also packed in high levels of nutrients to fight off oxidative stress.*

    - There have been studies producing evidence that taking supplements containing Cantaloupe's antioxidants may reduce the risk of lung, prostate, and other types of cancer.

## What food can reduce tumor?

Curcumin appears to **reduce tumor** reproduction, **reduce** blood vessel formation, **reduce** invasion and induce **tumor** cell death.

- **Curcumin** is the active ingredient in turmeric, a rhizome that's a member of the ginger family.

    - Turmeric is commonly used for conditions involving pain and *inflammation*, (*my issue*) such as osteoarthritis. It is also works for hay fever, depression, high cholesterol, a type of liver disease and itching.

- **Curcumin** supplements and capsules are the most efficient way to introduce **curcumin** into your diet.

    - Many supplements also have extra ingredients such as piperine (black pepper) to enhance absorption. For the dosage, Arthritis Foundation recommends 500 milligrams twice a day.

    - In one study, turmeric was more effective at inhibiting the growth of breast cancer cells than curcumin alone.

- Researchers found a similar trend with other tumor cells, suggesting that **curcumin** may not be the only potent plant compound in **turmeric**.

- **Ginger.**
  - Whether used as a fresh root or ground powder, ginger can provide benefit for the *lung cancer patient*.
  - Ginger has been shown to help relieve or lessen the severity of nausea.
  - Use this in sauces, marinades, soups, teas and stir-fry dishes (with added Tofu Protein) is a great way to incorporate it.

**You should take advantage of liquid Aminos benefits.**

- They contain amino acids. Amino acids are the building blocks of proteins. ...
- Naturally **gluten-free**. ...
- Milder taste than soy sauce. ...
- Don't contain chemical preservatives. ...
- May reduce hunger. ...
- Easy to add to your diet.

**Coconut aminos** can be *used exactly* as you would use soy sauce or tamari. This can be found on most grocery market shelves. (*hint*: look for **Bragg's** Amino - it is Gluten Free and much lower in MSG and Sodium than Soy sauce)

- You can substitute (**Bragg's**) Liquid Aminos with a ratio of 1:1 in any recipe that calls for soy sauce. If you need a thicker consistency such as would be provided by adding

Tamari to a sauce, whisk in a little bit of flour, corn starch, or arrowroot, depending on the cooking method.

- What Are **Liquid Aminos**, and can they benefit your health?

  - Liquid Amino's are culinary seasonings that look and taste similar to soy sauce.

  - They can be made by fermenting coconut sap with salt and water like treating soybeans with an acidic solution to break them down into free amino acids.

  - They add a savory, salty flavor to meals and are naturally vegan and gluten-free.

*Here are the benefits of liquid Amino's.*

- Amino acids are the building blocks of proteins.

- They are very important for building muscle, regulating gene expression, cell signaling, and immunity.

- There are two types of amino acids — essential and non-essential.

- Your body can produce non-essential amino acids, but essential amino acids can only be obtained from your diet.

- Manufacturers claim that soy-based liquid aminos contain 16 amino acids, while coconut-based ones offer 17, including both essential and non-essential. However, no independent research supports these claims.

### *Coconut Aminos are naturally gluten-free*

- Soy sauce is made by fermenting cooked soybeans and roasted wheat with salt, water, and yeast or mold until a rich, salty sauce is produced.

- In contrast, liquid Aminos are made by mixing hydrolyzed soybeans or fermented coconut sap with water, resulting in a naturally gluten-free product.

- Thus, those following a gluten-free diet commonly use them in place of soy sauce.

- Since roughly 5% of the world cannot eat gluten due to gluten-related disorders, liquid Aminos are a useful product for many people.

- Additionally, coconut Aminos are particularly popular among people following the paleo diet, as they cannot eat legumes like soybeans.

- Nonetheless, for recipes that involve reducing a sauce, coconut Aminos are a good choice, as they won't become overwhelmingly salty.

- Don't contain chemical preservatives

- Commercially prepared soy sauces often contain sodium benzoate.

  - Sodium benzoate is a preservative that's added to foods to increase their shelf life and prevent the growth of bacteria and fungi.

  - While it's generally recognized as safe when consumed in small quantities, some people are allergic to it, finding that it may trigger hives, itching, swelling, or runny nose.

- The Flavor profile of Aminos are Umami taste elements that are one of the five major taste sensations, alongside salty, sweet, sour, and bitter.

- Its flavor is described as savory or meaty and triggered by the presence of free glutamate. Free glutamate is formed in foods when glutamic acid, an amino acid naturally found in protein, is broken down.

- Liquid Aminos contain natural glutamate due to the breakdown of proteins in soybeans or coconut sap, so they stimulate an umami flavor sensation and make food taste more enjoyable.

- Research has found that consuming umami-flavored broths and soups before meals can reduce feelings of hunger and decrease the desire to snack.

*One study examined the brain activity of women who tended to overeat at meals.*

- When the women drank chicken broth containing monosodium glutamate (MSG), a food additive rich in glutamate and umami flavor, they showed greater brain activity in regions responsible for self-control while viewing images of food and making dietary decisions.

## Why is soy bad for you?

**Soy**, it turned out, contains estrogen-like compounds called isoflavones. And some findings suggested that these compounds could promote the growth of some cancer cells, impair female fertility, and mess with thyroid function.

**Soy** protein is a complete source of protein. It may aid muscle building but not as well as whey protein. Overall, **soy** is safe for most people and may offer health benefits, including **weight loss**.

**Does soy sauce have gluten?**

Traditionally, **soy sauce** is made from four main ingredients: soybeans, **wheat**, salt and water. Wheat is the source of gluten.

# Meat

## and our healthcare:

Proteins are the most important part of our diets to build a healthy person.

- Americans consume currently 111 grams of protein (mostly beef of course) a day.
    - Men only need 58 grams a day
    - And Women only need 46 grams per day.

Higher intake of red meats (beef the most offensive) irrespective of its fat content, increases the risk to heart disease, stokes and diabetes.

- When compared to fish, poultry, nuts and legumes (beans), they are slightly less potent in protein yet much better in fat content.

One in **ten deaths** in America could be ***prevented*** if you substitute half your normal intake of beef and replace with more starch and veggies for the entire meal's content.

- *So having a 4 oz. piece of beef on your plate is better than eating the usual American standard of 8 oz. steak size.*

In 2010 Americans used twice as many antibiotics to raise cows, chickens and pigs.[12]

- This has led to Americans having a resistance to (antibiotic) drugs used to protect us.

## Animal vs. Plant-based Protein's Footprint

It is commonly known that animal proteins are the basis for most of our daily food consumption.

*As Americans, it is thought you have to eat big portions of steaks, burgers and hot dogs.*

As a general rule, research has found that people can consume plant-based proteins and stay as healthy as anyone eating an animal based protein diet.

- Research has also shown that a plant-based diet has fewer calories and naturally becomes a better option for choices on your dinner plate.

Also, as a general ideal, animal protein-based foods take so much more in the way of the carbon footprint.

- It takes 4 times as many natural resources (food and growth needs) to produce as much animal protein content as plant-based content.[13]

---

12   https://www.ncbi.nlm.nih.gov/pmc/articles/PMC3234384/
13   https://academic.oup.com/ajcn/article/78/3/660S/4690010

- Animal protein has an equally bad mortality rate when Americans eat our currently accepted diet regime.

Here is a small comparison for alternative protein sources:

| Vegan proteins | Protein content/100 grams of total weight: |
|---|---|
| Potato | 2.5 grams |
| Spinach | 2.9 grams |
| Quinoa | 4.4 grams |
| Lima beans | 7.8 grams |
| Garbanzo Beans | 8.9 grams |
| Lentils | 9.0 grams |
| Pecans | 9.5 grams |
| Soybeans | 13.1 grams |
| Walnuts | 15. grams |
| Chai seeds | 15.6 grams |
| Oats | 16.9 grams |
| Tofu | 17.2 grams |
| Flaxseed | 19.5 grams |
| Almonds | 22 grams |
| Hemp seed | 23. grams |
| Peanut butter | 25 grams |
| Pumpkin seeds | 33 grams |

# *What is a Protein-Flip*

What's a *Protein-Flip*? It is rethinking how we learned to eat....I grew up normally eating a huge 8 oz. portion of beef and 2 oz. of veggies and 3 or 4 oz. of a starch.

We are suggesting you should now flip those portions.

- Have a 2 to 3 oz. cooked portion of meat.

- Decoratively paired with an interesting veggie combination that brings with it tastes and textures that could include a second veggie choice as a purée or prepared as the sauce.

- Having one or two choices in the starch content can also be doubled to give you a more full feeling after you finish your dinner.
    - Using a starch as an entrée food wrap (like a potato shell or a tortilla wrap).
    - Then you can have an interesting and tasty risotto as a base to elevate the presentation factor of the plate's look.

- Use meat as a condiment or seasoning in a mostly plant-based meal.

- Blend beef with other "better" proteins (like chicken / turkey) to compose a meal. (i.e…. meat loafs)

- Use limited protein content of beef in Surf and Turf meals.

- Add these to bring protein level of your meal to a total **Protein-Flip**:
    - Whole grains (i.e. … Faro)
    - Legume-based pastas
    - Rice and starch (potato) bowls
    - Tapas based with olives, nuts and other high-quality protein sources.

# Here are some basic generalities of Beef vs. Plant-based protein source:

|  | Lentils | vs. | Ground beef |
|---|---|---|---|
|  | per 100 grams |  | per 100 grams |
| Calories | 358 |  | 137 |
| Carbs | 63 grams |  | 0 grams |
| Proteins | 23,9 grams |  | 21.4 grams |
| Fats | 2.2 grams ( no trans fats) |  | 5 grams (and Tans fats) |
| Fiber | 10.8 grams |  | 0 grams |
| Cholesterol | 0 mg |  | 62 mg |
| Iron | 7,4 grams |  | 2.4 gm |

And, to make these changes easier, try these ideas...

*These choices and changes in our diet are not only going to make your meals less expensive but, it usually boasts flavor-profiles that creates a more interesting dining experience.*

Pair these choices with hunger-satisfying sauces and condiments.

- IE... cremas, guacamole, salsas, flavored oils, coulis and "*Coulis-grette*s[14]"

There have been studies in recipe flavor profiles that say that mushrooms have become a great **Protein-flip** enhancer and balancer.

- Mushrooms when substituted for meats in a recipe give you a similar taste profile. This is where the "Vegan" burger gets its tasty quality.

---
14      https://ar.pinterest.com/pin/221380137903022790/

- Mushrooms can be substituted for beef in:
  - Shepherds pies, meat loafs, tacos, lasagna, pasta sauces, fillings for Italian, French and Latino favorite dishes (i.e....manicotti, crêpes and burritos)
    - Saturated fats in a recipe can be reduced by as much as one-third using mushrooms.

## And for Saturated fats…..

As Americans, we generally have as many health-related issues associated with saturated fat as it relates to heart disease and cancer. I have found that they are both serious issues that can be *inter-related*.

Most deaths in my family tree have stemmed from one or the other and sometimes both occurring to my closest relatives.

- One of the things that I have found to be a generally accepted healthy alternative in modern dining is the use of margarine instead of butter.
- This is and has been debunked and here is why. Butter has cholesterol of course. Margarine naturally doesn't --- because it is made from oils.

What hasn't been stated in most margarine's marketing efforts (it's *health halo*) is to advertise margarine as a better alternative to butter. Margarine that is solid at room temperature is **saturated**. Saturated fats are more than a bad choice, they also have trans-fats.

- Trans-fats cause spikes in Cholesterol.

- Trans-fats raise LDL while lowering HDL (good cholesterol levels)

*In general, it is my opinion and others that foods cooked with limited amounts of organic or grass-fed butters are less hazardous to your health.*

## Food Sources of Fatty Acids

After going through this wide array of fatty acids, you may be wondering where they are found in nature.

The figure below shows the fatty acid composition of certain oils and oil-based foods. As you can see, most foods contain a mixture of fatty acids.

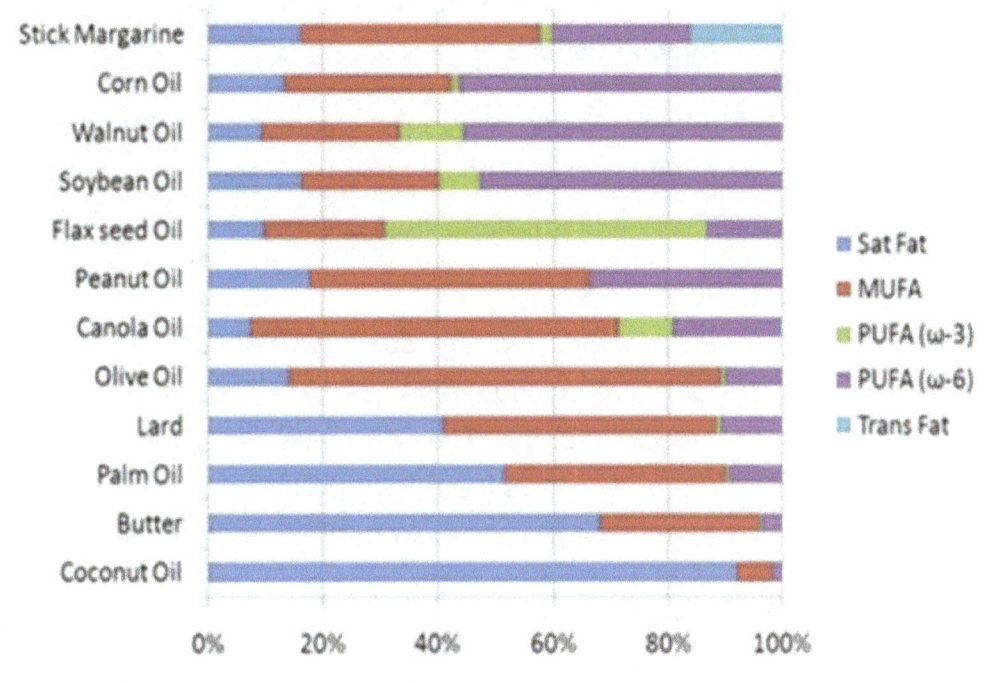

Fatty acid composition of foods and oils

To discuss this chart further, this chart will help you decide what you want to use to cook with, or enhance your foods' tastes. It is easy to see how healthy fats can be chosen. Any oil high in MUFA and PUFA[15] are preferred by most experts for cooking your meals. And this chart can help you decide which oils to use compared to what product advertising tells you...

---

15   https://www.netmeds.com/health-library/post/all-about-pufa-and-mufa-functions-and-health-benefits

- **Saturated Fats** (sat Fat) are represented by the blue line.

- **MUFA** are Mono-saturated fatty acids represented by the red line

  - *Mono-unsaturated fatty acids (MUFAs) are a healthy type of fat. Replacing less healthy fats, such as saturated fats and trans fats, with unsaturated fats, such as MUFAs and polyunsaturated fats, may offer health benefits.*

- **PUFA** (Omega-3 and 6 fats) Polyunsaturated fatty acids are a type of fat in certain foods. Omega -3 and 6 fatty acids studies have found these components of a healthy dining lifestyle.

  - *Polyunsaturated fatty acids (PUFAs) are important for nerve function, blood clotting, brain health, and muscle strength. They are "essential," meaning that the body needs them to function but cannot make them, so a person must get PUFAs from their diet.*

- **Trans fats** raise your bad (LDL[16]) cholesterol levels and lower your good (HDL) cholesterol levels. Eating trans fats increases your risk of developing heart disease and stroke. It's also associated with a higher risk of developing type 2 diabetes.

---

16   https://medlineplus.gov/ldlthebadcholesterol.html

# Chapter Two:

*Recipes*

# *The Beginning:*

*M*y new philosophy in the kitchen is a word christened:

## *"Kaizen"*

...this means good change, or continuous improvement, in the Japanese language.

*In other words:*

## *"Improve Health with Food"*

*We are now cooking and eating in a style that emphasizes and celebrates, but is not limited to, plant-based foods—including fruits and vegetables, whole grains, beans, legumes (pulses), soy foods, nuts and seeds, plant oils, and herbs and spices.*

To help you communicate the many terms in the plant-forward family ... from "flexitarian" to "vegan" .

The plant-forward movement is showing up in kitchens across the country. Here are the concepts taking veggie-rich dining to the next level. We are using this premise to develop a closer to the ground. "Earth-Centric" cuisine that has been known to help entire cultures of peoples to live a longer life.

# What do we use in place of animal proteins when we talk about plant-forward?

It is an Earth or Plant forward Strategy.

...An Asian plant forward strategy is to use handfuls of herbs;

> ....to build savory notes,
>
> ....to enhance herbaceous-ness,
>
> ...building a more spice forward taste-profile...

Vietnamese and Korean cuisines are spiritual. They have been built around the fact that each food element deserves respect and it shows in the way they create recipes.

- Vegetarian cuisines are mostly from Asian descent. Vegetarianism is less expensive overall, so you will see "plant-forward" recipes in most lower economically developed cultures.

- Aromatics; fresh herbs, become the main ingredient in this menu theory.

    - Contrast of flavors makes for a showcase of products.

    - Smokey, sticky, textures ... proteins are a secondary concern in this theory of recipe development.

Different stages of ripeness or quality can become a "Study-in" and of veggies.

- Dried, (one day drying-*new trend*)

- Fermented,

- Cutting specifics,

- Combinations of; and in-between,

- Textures of veggies,
- Bruising veggies, that release their juices,
  - to celebrate veggies on the plate!

*Heat spices first in the pan before cooking!*

*Use handfuls of herbs instead of teaspoons.*

> Plant-forward dishes can include animal proteins. Those who eat a plant-forward diet—many of whom self-identify as *flexitarian*—generally consume large amounts of fresh produce, whole grains, pulses, beans, and nuts but are not locked into an exclusively plant-based regimen.

....*Plant-forward* implies: dietary and food system transformation that includes a whole range of healthier, more sustainable approaches—from those that contain poultry, fish, dairy, and/or small amounts of meat to vegetarian and vegan offerings.

In reality, when we talk about plant-forward, we talk about a massive variety of diets, recipes, chefs and restaurants. Vegan and vegetarian fare are part of it, but so too are dishes that creatively marry plants with smaller servings of animal protein.

*Consistent small actions, repeated over time, add up to big results.*

Plant-based diet: Some define this as "plants only." But our definition is broader. For us, plant-based diets consist mostly of plants: vegetables, fruits, beans/legumes, whole grains, nuts, and seeds. In other words, if you consume mostly plants with some animal-based protein, we would still consider you a plant-based eater.

Whole-food plant-based diet: A type of plant-based diet that emphasizes whole, minimally processed foods.

Fully plant-based / plant-only diet: These eating patterns include only foods from the plant/fungi kingdom without any animal products. Fully plant-based eaters don't consume meat or meat products, dairy, or eggs. Some consume no animal byproducts at all—including honey.

Vegan diet: A type of strict, fully plant-based diet that tends to include broader lifestyle choices such as not wearing fur or leather. Vegans often attempt to avoid actions that bring harm or suffering to animals.

Vegetarian diet: "Vegetarian" is an umbrella term that includes plant-only diets (fully plant-based / plant-only / vegan) as well as several other plant-based dining patterns:

Lacto-ovo vegetarians consume dairy and eggs.

Pesco-pollo vegetarians eat fish, shellfish, and chicken.

Pescatarians eat fish and shellfish.

Flexitarians eat mostly plant foods as well as occasional, small servings of meat. A self-described flexitarian seeks to decrease meat consumption without eliminating it entirely.

Omnivore: Someone who consumes a mix of animals and plants.

*Now we can say: after a consensus of research we now know what these terms mean...*

*Example, when researchers in Belgium asked nearly 1500 vegans, vegetarians, semi-vegetarians, pescatarians, and omnivores about their food intake, they found that fully plant-based eaters scored highest on the Healthy Eating Index, which is a measure of dietary quality.*

Omnivores (people who eat at least some meat) scored lowest on the Healthy Eating Index and the other groups scored somewhere in between. Meat eaters were also more likely than other groups to be overweight or obese.

Other research has also linked vegetarian diets with better health indicators, ranging from blood pressure to waist circumference.

Since it takes work—label reading, food prep, menu scrutiny—to follow this eating style, they may also be more conscious of their food intake, which leads to healthier choices (plant-based eaters also tend to sleep more and watch less TV, which can also boost health).

And meat-eaters score lower not because they eat meat, but because of a low intake of whole foods such as fish and seafood, fruit, beans, nuts, and seeds. They also have a higher intake of refined grains and sodium.

Meat-eaters, other research shows, also tend to drink and smoke more than plant-based eaters.

In other words, meat may not be the problem. A diet loaded with highly-processed "foods" and virtually devoid of whole, plant foods, on the other hand, is a problem.

Nutritional Recommendations international consortium, made up of 14 researchers in seven countries, published five research reviews based on 61 population studies of more than 4 million participants, along with several randomized trials, to discern the link between red meat consumption and disease.

800 studies, the International Agency for Research on Cancer (IARC), a part of the World Health Organization, determined that each daily 50-gram portion of processed meat[17]—roughly the amount of one hot dog or six slices of cooked bacon—*increased risk of colon cancer by 18 percent.*

They listed red meat as "probably carcinogenic" and processed red meat as "carcinogenic," putting it in the same category as smoking and alcohol.

---

17   https://www.who.int/news-room/q-a-detail/cancer-carcinogenicity-of-the-consumption-of-red-meat-and-processed-meat

Relative risk: The likelihood something (such as cancer) will happen when a new variable (such as red meat) is added to a group, compared to a group of people who don't add that variable.

Absolute risk: The amount that something (such as red meat) will raise your total risk of developing a problem (such as cancer) over time.

Smoking. Smoking doubles your risk of dying in the next 10 years[18]. Smoking, by the way, also accounts for 30 percent of all cancer deaths, killing more Americans than alcohol, car accidents, suicide, AIDS, homicide, and illegal drugs combined

---

18   https://www.ncbi.nlm.nih.gov/books/NBK126159/

# Recipes:

## *Delectable Delights*

### *Something lite with a with a little added Spice:*

Asian seasoning blends in addition to having well balanced textures and flavors are also visually appealing. ... The spices that are typically used in Asian cuisine are truly helpful in the fight of Cancer issues. These include: cassia (cinnamon), cilantro, coriander (seeds), (hot) chilies, cloves, cumin, galangal (similar to ginger), garlic, ginger, lemongrass, star anise and turmeric.

✷✷✷✷

# Curry Paste

*This recipe brings all the best Cancer fighting spices together for a simple paste that can flavor soups, sauce and a base for marinades.*

**Ingredients:**

| | |
|---|---|
| 4 Tbs. | Coriander seeds |
| 2 Tbs. | Cumin |
| 1 Tbs. | Fenugreek seeds |
| 1 Tbs. | Fennel seeds |
| 2 each | Curry leaves |
| 2 each | Red chilies, dried |
| 2 Tsp. | Turmeric |
| 2 Tsp. | Chili powder |
| 5 Tbs. | White wine vinegar |
| 2 Tbs. | Water |
| ½ Cup | Oil |

**Directions:**

Grind the first 6 ingredients in a spice grinder. Process them smooth. Add the spices. Grind well again. Form a paste.

Heat the oil in a skillet. Add this paste and cook for 10 minutes. Add the water and liquids. Cook until the oil rises to the top of the mixture. Cool.

*Store this recipe in a glass jar for up to 2 months.*

# Indonesian Spice ....for Tuna loins or for using in a seared Chicken breast recipe.

*This might be the most generic spice blend in modern Indonesian cooking for today. \*\*\*Use this as a 3 hour marinade for lighter proteins (turkey, seafood, etc…).*

**Ingredients:**

| | |
|---|---|
| 1 each | Cinnamon stick |
| 8 each | Chilies, dried |

| | |
|---|---|
| 5 Tbs. | Coriander seeds |
| 2 Tbs. | Cumin seeds |
| 1 Tbs. | Cardamom seeds |
| 1 Tsp. | Fennel seeds |
| 1 Tsp. | Mustard seeds |
| 2 Tsp. | Black peppercorns |
| 1 Tsp. | Cloves, whole |

**Directions:**

Warm the spices first in a preheated skillet to get the oils from the seeds which makes the blend more fragrant. Continue cooking in the pan until you notice smoking seeds begin to pop. Cool. Grind when well cooled in a spice grinder.

*Store this recipe in a glass jar for up to 3 months.*

# Asian Spice blend

*This can be associated with a product commercially made called "Chinese Five Spice". This blend is used in the Asian countries as we use Salt and pepper here in the America. \*\*\*I find it can make boring foods interesting. Try it on French fries one day and then use it on roasted pork the next to see how these spices change your opinion on everyday seasonings.*

**Ingredients:**

| | |
|---|---|
| ¼ Cup | Onion powder |
| ¼ Cup | Garlic powder |
| ¼ Cup | Black pepper, ground fine |
| 2 Tbs. | Ginger powder, ground |
| 1 Tsp. | Anise pods, ground fine |
| 2 Tbs. | Red pepper flakes |

***Optional:***
| | |
|---|---|
| 1 Tsp. | Sugar, for grilled foods. |

**Directions:**

Grind all ingredients well in a spice grinder. Blend all smooth.

*Store in a glass jar for up to 2 months.*


# Spicy Asian Paste

*... for ribs and grilled chicken.*

**Ingredients:**

| | |
|---|---|
| 3 Tbs. | Oil |
| 3 each | Shallots, finely chopped |
| 3 cloves | Garlic, finely chopped |
| 2 Tbs. | Cilantro, chopped |
| 2 each | Thai Chiles, seeded and finely chopped |
| 3 Tbs. | Ginger, finely chopped fresh |
| 2 Tbs. | Curry powder |
| ½ Tsp. | Nutmeg, ground |
| 2 each | Star anise |
| 8 each | Plums, purple, ripe, pitted and coarsely chopped |
| ¼ Cup | Rice wine vinegar |
| 1 Tbs. | Asian Sesame oil |
| 1 Tbs. | Agave syrup |

**Directions:**

Heat the oil in a skillet. Add the shallots and garlic. Slowly warm both until they soften yet not brown.

Add the spices and stir in well. Let them cook for 3 minutes. Then add the plums and cook for another 3 minutes, breaking up the fruit into pulp.

Add the other liquids and cook until the paste forms into a soft-creamy solution.

Add to foods as they are cooking on your grill as long as you are slow cooking. I use this on turkey tenderloins as well. (Use the tenderloins sliced cold and served atop a salad).

Use for rubbing onto ribs or chicken cooked on your grill.

I have tried it on Pacific salmon as well brushing the paste onto the fillets just before you are ready to serve.

# Macha Vinaigrette- Marinade

*Note: This recipe is for those looking for a seasoning blend that boasts a lot of extra protein in this recipe. This unusual one can be your favorite. It is great as a marinade, dressing, side dish enhancer, atop a salad or Tuna loin. It is not limited to being used as a sauce. I find it great for steak-cut seafood like Swordfish, Wahoo or Kingfish (King Mackerel).*

## Ingredients:

| | |
|---|---|
| 1.5 Cup | Oil |
| 4 each | Garlic crushed |
| 2 Tbs. | Brown sugar |
| 2 each | Chipotle chili, canned and Chipotle sauce from can |
| 1 lb. | Cashews, 1/2 rough chopped and, 1/2 pulverize well |
| 15 stalks | Cilantro, fresh |
| 1 Tsp. | Salt |

\*\*\*

| | |
|---|---|
| 3 oz. | Apple Cider vinegar |
| 1 oz. | Apple jack brandy |
| 4 oz. | EVO |

## Directions:

Lightly simmer the garlic in oil. Brown slightly. On low heat, stir in the sugar and chilies. Let simmer and stir well for 5 minutes so flavors meld and combine. Add the nuts and keep stirring the whole time. Cook another 3 minutes so nuts thicken the mix.

Off heat add the cilantro and salt if needed. Store as a paste until you decide to make the vinaigrette.

 \*\*\* Add the last three ingredients to make the vinaigrette. Place the paste in a food processor and add the ingredients one at a time.

Use for salads or a sauce for all kinds of grilled foods or a topping for tacos and quesadillas. Use cold or warm atop seafood and beef and pork steaks .

\* Use the rough chopped nuts as garnish on top the cooked food.

I have used this with tuna and two sauces. Red one is a roasted **red pepper puree** and the other is a **Dijon-Coconut aioli** that follows.

# Roasted Red Pepper and Pineapple

Serves: 4-6

## Ingredients:

| | |
|---|---|
| 1 Tbs. | Garlic, roasted, crushed |
| 12 oz. | Roasted red bell peppers, canned, drained |
| 4 oz. | Pineapple, grilled, cooled |
| 2 oz. | Lime juice |
| 1 Tbs. | Thai chili sauce |
| 1 Tsp. | Salt |
| 2 oz. | EVO |
| 1 oz. | Coconut milk |

## Directions:

Place the first six ingredients in a blender and process smooth. Add the rest of the ingredients. Check seasonings. Keep at room temperature.

# Dijon Lime Coconut Aioli

Serves: 6

## Ingredients:

| | |
|---|---|
| 1 Tbs. | Garlic, roasted, crushed |
| 4 Tbs. | Dijon mustard |
| 2 oz. | Lime juice |
| 1 Tsp. | Salt |
| 2 oz. | EVO |
| 4 oz. | Mayonnaise |
| 3 oz. | Coconut cream/milk, *the cream that rises to the top* |

## Directions:

Blend everything together. Add more coconut if you like. I like more for seafood and salads.

# Coconut, Lime, Chili Seafood Marinade

Serves: 6

**Ingredients:**

| | |
|---|---|
| 4 oz. | Coconut milk, no cream (*just clear milk*) |
| 2 oz. | Lime juice |
| 4 Tbs. | Garlic, crushed fine |
| 2 Tbs. | Thai chili sauce |
| 1 Tbs. | Cilantro, fine chopped |
| 1 Tbs. | Fish sauce |
| 2 oz. | Soursop, puree |
| 4 oz. | Papaya puree |
| 1 Tsp. | Salt |
| 2 Tbs. | Coconut Aminos |
| 2 oz. | EVO |

**Directions:**

Mix all ingredients and use to marinate fish and seafood before cooking.

\*\*\*Use this for a **sauce** base if you cook this marinade (and it will thicken as it cooks) and used as a cold salad dressing or on seafood. I have served it here if a medium-rare, pan-seared **Wahoo**.

**For the Wahoo dish:** *(see picture that follows)*

Use 5 oz. steak of Wahoo per person.

Season the steaks as you like, use the above recipe as a marinade. Heat a heavy bottom pan very hot. Place the steaks in the pan a few at a time. Seared about 3 minutes per side for a 2 inch cut fillets.

Cool slightly before slicing the steaks 4 times and then place the slices around veggies (or rice) and drizzle sauce around on the plate.

*See picture next page...*

*Wahoo*

# Dhal ~ This recipe is for anyone that loves hummus.

Dhal is simple to make and tastes even better the day after, so it makes a convenient, healthy, quick-reheat dinner for busy schedules.

This is what my wife has said is the best recipe for every issue you don't want to deal with for cooking for people with Cancer.

It is easy to crock pot this recipe and it is easily re-heatable for leftover the next day.

A great gluten-free recipe stock full of grains and the tasty spice factor is medium heat ratio.

We like to make the spice blend in bulk as it can be used in lots of dishes. Use as a spice like Za'atar.

You can use for spreads and compound butter to be used as a topping for grilled foods.

## Ingredients:

*First part of recipe: Spice mix...*

| | |
|---|---|
| 1 Tsp. | Ginger powder |
| 2 Tbs. | Chili flakes |
| 1 each | Bay leaf |
| 3 each | Cloves |
| 1 Tbs. | Coriander seeds |
| 1 Tbs. | Caraway seeds |
| 3 each | Cardamom pods |
| 1 each | Cinnamon quill |
| 1 Tsp. | Cumin seeds |
| ½ Tsp. | Fenugreek |
| 2 Tsp. | Turmeric powder |
| 1 Tsp. | Fennel seeds |
| ½ Tsp. | Black peppercorns |
| 1 Tsp. | Mustard, ground |
| ½ Cup | Curry leaves, fresh |

## Second recipe; Dhal:

| | |
|---|---|
| 3 Tbs. | Oil |
| 2 each | Onion, chopped, browned in oil |
| 5 cloves | Garlic, chopped |
| ½ Cup | Quinoa |
| ½ Cup | Yellow split peas |
| ½ Cup | Green split peas |
| ½ Cup | Amaranth |

| | |
|---|---|
| 2 qt. | Vegetable stock |
| To taste | Seasalt |
| 8 oz. | Peas, frozen |
| 7 oz. | Greek Yogurt |
| ½ bunch | Mint |
| 1 each | Lemon |

**Directions:**

In a heavy-bottom frying pan, roast all the spices for three to five minutes on medium heat or till they start to smoke. Remove from heat, cool and blend in a coffee mill. *Store extra spice for any additional recipes you want to perk up.* We like to put it on top of hummus.

In the same pan on a high heat, add the oil and fry the onions and garlic until soft. Add three heaping tablespoons of spice mix and cook for another three to four minutes, stirring constantly. Brown the onions being careful not to burn.

Add the quinoa, split peas, and amaranth and stir for a few minutes. Then start adding the stock gradually, stirring, until the grains are covered and the stock is simmering. Keep adding stock as the Dhal absorbs it, stir, as though you are making risotto, for about 15-20 minutes until the grains have softened, but still have a little bite.

Drain the peas well. Season the Dhal with salt, add half the peas and half the yogurt and stir through.

### *To serve,*

Spoon the Dhal into bowls, drizzle over the remaining yogurt after you stir the creamed yogurt well making it runny, top with peas and mint leaves and a squeeze of lemon juice. Serve with Naan bread or chips.

# Ancho-onion Jam

*Great recipe to use for several dishes. That is why it is a larger batch.*

Serves: 12

## Ingredients:

| | |
|---|---|
| As needed | EVO |
| 4 lbs. | Onion, sliced (weep slowly to soften) |
| 1 can | Ancho chilies, small can |
| 2 oz. | Garlic, crushed |
| 3 oz. | Balsamic syrup |
| As needed | Salt |
| 1 lb. | "Fake" bacon, chopped |
| .5 Cup | Aguve syrup |
| .3 Cup | Water |
| 2 # | Veggie sausage |
| 1 bunch | Cilantro, chopped |

## Directions:

Sauté the onions then reduce heat to a simmer until they are soft and almost mushy. Add the other veggies, fake bacon and sausage. Let simmer for 30 minutes.

Season. Add the cilantro and water. Raise the temperature to a boil and continue to stir and cook until almost dry and syrupy.

***Use atop the Pork Schnitzel recipe found later in the book.

# General Tao's Tofu

Servings: 4

**Ingredients:**

| | |
|---|---|
| 1 box | Tofu, firm (16 ounce) |
| 1 each | Egg |
| ¾ Cup | Cornstarch |
| As needed | Vegetable oil (for frying) |
| 3 each | Green onions, chopped |
| 1 Tbs. | Ginger, minced |
| 1 Tbs. | Garlic, minced |
| ⅔ Cup | Vegetable stock |
| 2 Tbs. | Tamari (*or Aminos*-see previous pages for more info.) |
| 4 Tbs. | Agave |
| To taste | Sriracha sauce |
| 1 Tbs. | Sherry wine |
| 1 Tbs. | Rice wine vinegar |

**Directions**:

Drain, dry and cut tofu into one inch chunks-You can freeze the tofu the night before. Mix egg with 3 Tbs. of water. Dip tofu in mixture. Sprinkle cornstarch over tofu to completely cover.

Heat oil in a pan and fry tofu pieces until golden brown and then set aside. Drain oil.

Heat 3 Tbs. Vegetable oil in a pan on medium heat and add onions, ginger and garlic, cook for about two minutes. Add vegetable stock, soy sauce, sugar, red pepper flakes and vinegar. Mix 2 Tbs. of water and 1 Tbs. Cornstarch and pour into mixture, stirring well. Thicken. Add fried tofu and coat evenly.

# Honey Mustard with Mango and Coconut

Serves: 6

### Ingredients:

| | |
|---|---|
| 2 oz. | Honey |
| 3 oz. | Dijon mustard |
| 3 oz. | Mango puree |
| 1/2 Tsp. | Fish sauce |
| 1 Tsp. | Sriracha sauce |
| 4 oz. | Coconut milk, include cream from the top |
| 2 oz. | Mayo |
| 1 Tsp. | Seasalt |

### Directions:

Mix all in a blender.

### *Notes:*

Use this for a glaze on fish fillets that are already grilled or baked.


# Pineapple-Mango Spread

Serves: 12

### Ingredients:

| | |
|---|---|
| .5 each | Pineapple, no husk, sliced |
| 2 each | Mango, sliced thin |
| 10 each | Sweet baby chilies |
| 10 stalks | Cilantro, chopped |
| 1 Tbs. | Salt |
| 1 Tsp. | Sriracha sauce |
| 3 oz. | Agave syrup |
| 2 Tbs. | Ginger, fine chopped |

**Directions:**

Add everything together simmer until thick and almost like a paste. Cool. Store in a jar for months

**Notes:**

Use for picnic baskets of chicken, seafood or a sandwich bread spread.


# Summer Corn and Coconut chowder

Serves: 4

**Ingredients:**

| | |
|---|---|
| 2 Tbs. | Coconut oil |
| 1 medium | Onion, yellow, diced |
| 1 each | Carrot, medium-size, diced |
| 2 cloves | Garlic, minced |
| 1 each | Jalapeño peppers, seeded and diced |
| 3 Cups | Corn kernels, fresh or frozen (thawed if frozen) |
| 1 each | Coconut milk, full-fat, (14-ounce can) |
| 3 Cups | Veggie stock, see notes |
| to taste | Salt and pepper 1 teaspoon fresh lime zest |
| 2 Tbs. | Lime juice, fresh |

<u>**Sub recipe**</u> - Toppings:

| | |
|---|---|
| 1/2 Cup | Cilantro, fresh, minced |
| 3 each | Jalapeños, pickled, sliced into thin rounds |
| 1/2 Cup | Corn kernels, fresh or frozen (thawed if frozen) |
| 3 Tbs. | Coconut flakes, unsweetened |

**Directions:**

Add the coconut oil to a large stock pot over medium-high heat. Once the oil is hot, add the onion and sauté until lightly browned and tender, about 5 minutes. Add the garlic, fresh jalapeños, and corn. Cook and stir often, until the vegetables are tender, about 5 minutes.

Stir in coconut milk and water. Bring to a boil. Reduce heat and simmer until the vegetables are soft and the soup is fragrant, about 15-20 minutes. Add salt and pepper to taste.

Use an immersion blender or, working in batches, carefully transfer the soup to a high-speed blender and purée until smooth.

Return the soup to the pot. Stir in the lime zest and juice. Taste and add additional salt and pepper if needed and garnish with plenty of minced cilantro, pickled jalapeños and corn as desired.

Ladle the soup into bowls and top with coconut flakes.

### ***Notes:***

*My wife's favorite short cut to flavor boosting a recipe is using a veggie stock instead of starting a recipe with water only. \*\*\*Veggie stock is the most useful way to make all your veggie trimmings not go to waste. Always take your trimmings and topping of carrots, onions, celery and other root veggies and bag them in your freezer. When you have a pound or more, put them in a pot filled with water and stew the scrap for at least 30 minutes. Strain, cool and store in your refrigerator to use within that same week or freeze and use as you like.*

# Black Bean bowls with Butternut Squash, Black rice, and Chimi-churry

Serves: 8

This recipe makes a lot, but the leftovers keep well. You can easily cut the recipe in half. We love it for our weekly neighborhood happy hours.

## Ingredients:

| | |
|---|---|
| 2 cans | Black bean, 15-ounce |
| 1 Tsp. | Cumin, ground |
| 1 Tsp. | Garlic powder |
| ½ Cup | Cilantro, chopped |
| 1 Cup | Butternut squash, precooked, (or left overs), chopped |
| 2 oz. | EVO |
| 3 Tsp. | Kosher salt |
| 1 Cup | Black Chinese rice, precooked, (or left overs) |
| ½ Cup | Red cabbage, shredded |
| ½ Cup | Black Kale, shredded, salted, drained for five minutes |
| 1 each | Ripe avocado, peeled and cut into chunks |
| ½ Cup | Tomato salsa, use as a garnish on top |
| ¼ Cup | Cilantro, Chopped fresh, use as a garnish |
| ¼ Cup | Cotija cheese, use as a garnish |
| 1 recipe | Chimi-churry, see recipe, drizzle over for flavor |

## Directions:

Precook the rice in 4+ cups of water. Preheat your oven to 375 degrees.

Toss the Squash with EVO and 2 Tsp. salt and roast for 20 minutes in a 375-degree oven. Remove from heat and cut to appropriate size for the bowl.

Mix together the rest of the ingredients except for the garnishing ingredients. Place in bowls and top decoratively with the salsa, cheese cilantro and drizzle over with the Chimi-churry.

### *Second recipe:* Chimi-churry Recipe

**Ingredients:**

| | |
|---|---|
| 1 Cup | Parsley, flat-leaf, trimmed of thick stems, firmly packed fresh |
| 3-4 each | Garlic cloves |
| 2 Tbs. | Oregano leaves, fresh |
| ⅓ Cup | EVO olive oil |
| 2 Tbs. | Red or Malt vinegar |
| 2 Tbs. | Lime juice |
| ½ Tsp. | Seasalt |
| ⅛ Tsp. | Black pepper, ground |
| ¼ Tsp. | Red pepper flakes |

**Directions:**

Finely chop the parsley, fresh oregano, and garlic with a knife.

**Or,** place in a food processor with 4 oz. of water added. Whirl the herbs, the water helps chop the herbs properly. Drain herbs and place in a kitchen rag, twist the ends up on the rag and squeeze out the excess water.

Place in a small bowl.

Stir in the olive oil, vinegar, lime juice, salt, pepper, and red pepper flakes.

Use right away.

# Healthy Sausage Brunch Frittata

**Ingredients:**

| | |
|---|---|
| 2 each | Sausage patties, Vegetarian Breakfast, classic |
| ½ small | Onion, sweet, cut into ½-inch thick slices |
| 1 Cup | Spinach, baby |
| 2 large | Eggs plus 3 large egg whites |
| ¼ Cup | Cheese, grated plant-based ((you can find at larger grocery stores now-such as (Swiss) Gruyère)) |
| 2 Tbs. | Almond milk |
| As needed | Sea salt |
| As needed | Black pepper, (or a dash of red pepper flakes) |
| As needed | Lettuces and herbs, baby, if you can get the name brand: *Little gem* |
| As needed | Extra-virgin olive oil and Lemon juice, for dressing salad greens |

**Directions:**

Place a 1.5-cup oven-proof baking dish on a rimmed baking sheet and place in oven; preheat oven to 450 degrees.

In a medium skillet, cook vegetarian Breakfast Sausage, from frozen, over medium-high heat until golden brown, about 2 minutes per side. Set aside and slice in quarters.

Reduce heat to medium, sauté onion until tender but slightly crisp, about 2-3 minutes. Add spinach; cook until wilted, about 2 minutes more. Season with salt and pepper.

In a medium bowl, whisk together eggs and egg whites, half the cheese, milk, 1/2 teaspoon salt, and 1/4 teaspoon of pepper. Stir in spinach mixture and vegetarian Breakfast Sausage into egg mixture.

Remove heated dish from oven. Immediately pour in egg mixture and top with remaining cheese and freshly cracked black pepper.

Bake until frittata is puffed up and golden brown, about 15 minutes.

In a medium bowl, toss little gems and herbs with oil and vinegar. Season with salt and pepper as you like.

Serve frittata immediately with dressed greens.

*Optional:*

Use the **Beet-mango relish** (page 168) as a side accompaniment.

# Peach, Leek and Roasted Peppers

Serves: 4

**Ingredients:**

| | |
|---|---|
| 1 Tsp. | Salt |
| 1 Tsp. | Red chili flakes |
| 2 Tbs. | Lime juice |
| 2 Tbs. | Agave |

\*\*\*

| | |
|---|---|
| 6 each | Peach, cleaned, sliced |
| 1 each | Leek, white part only, thin sliced |
| ½ Cup | Roasted red Peppers, jully |
| 12 each | Grape cherry tomatoes, ½'ed |
| 20 each | Chive batons, ¾ inch pieces |
| 1 Cup | Kale, baby |

\*\*\*\*

| | |
|---|---|
| 3 oz. | Goat's cheese crumbles, per plate |
| 2 oz. | Grape must, find in specialty Italian market store |
| 4 oz. | EVO |

**Directions:**

Clean the peaches and mix with the first half the recipe. Let rest 20 minutes.

Mix with rest of the salad ingredients and place on separate plates.

Arrange the tomatoes and chive batons decoratively on the plates. Top with Goat cheese and then mix the Grape must and EVO drizzle over the plates.

# Cucumber Wasabi Sesame Salad

Serves: 4

**Ingredients:**

| | |
|---|---|
| 2 each | European cucumbers, thin cut on bias |
| 4 oz. | Rice wine vinegar |
| 1 tsp. | Sesame seeds, black and white, each |
| 1 Tbs. | Sesame oil |
| ½ Tsp. | Wasabi powder |
| 2 Tsp. | Salt |
| 1 Tbs. | Agave syrup |
| ½ each | Onion, red, jully |
| 2 Cup | Arugula, baby |
| As needed | Micro cilantro |

**Directions:**

Clean and slice cucumbers. Season the cucumbers with salt and wasabi. Let stand 20 minutes, then drain the cucumbers well. Mix the liquids for the dressing, add the seeds and then toss with cucumbers.

Remove from dressing and add to arugula, onions and place on plate and garnish with micro cilantro.

# Golden Beet Salad

Serves: 4

**Ingredients:**

| | |
|---|---|
| 2 each | Baby Iceberg lettuce, hallowed (to form a bowl) |
| 1 each | Golden beet pickled, sliced thin, See recipe |
| ½ each | White onion, julienned |
| 1 doz. | Chives, cut into 4 inch Batons and chop the rest |
| 2 Tbs. | EVO |
| 2 Tbs. | Coconut flakes, toasted |
| 12 each | Cherry tomato, halved |
| 2 each | Radish, cut into batons |
| 1 recipe | Coconut water syrup, see following recipe |

**Directions:**

Hallow the baby Iceberg lettuce by cutting base and pulling out lettuce core.

Mix the pickled beets onion and syrup. Fill lettuce garnish with more chives and toasted coconut. Place the tomatoes halves, radish and chive batons around the base of the salad. Take a small amount of the pickling brine and mix with EVO. Use it as the salads dressing for the base of the salad.

**Pickled golden beets**

| | |
|---|---|
| 2 each | Beets, 1\4'ed |
| 1 each | Onion, sliced |
| 2 each | Bay leaf |
| 1 Tbs | Curry spice |
| 1 Tbs. | Ginger powder |
| 4 Tbs. | Sugar |
| 4 Tsp. | Salt |
| 1 Cup. | Rice wine vinegar |
| As needed | Water |

**Directions:**

Mix all. Cover with water and boil till beets are soft enough to pierce with a fork. About 25 minutes.

Drain a little water fill with ice to cool rapidly.

Store in back of refrigerator for up to 6 months

**Coconut syrup**

| | |
|---|---|
| 4 oz. | Water from coconut |
| 4 oz. | Agave syrup |
| As need | Salt |
| Dash | Vanilla syrup |

Cook all ingredients in a heavy bottom pot till the sauce thickens like honey. Drizzle over the salad as a dressing.

# Asparagus, Peaches and Tomatoes Salad

Serves: 4

**Ingredients:**

| | |
|---|---|
| ½ bunch | Asparagus, cut on the bias, blanched, (learn the process from the charred beans recipe) |
| 1 Cup | Cherry tomatoes, three color, ½'ed |
| 1 each | English cucumber, de-seed, sliced on the bias |
| 2 each | Baby chilies, thin sliced |
| 2 each | Peach, slightly under-ripe, sliced thin |
| 2 each | Lime juice |
| 2 Tbs. | EVO |
| 1 Tsp. | Salt |
| 2 Tbs. | Cilantro, chopped |
| As needed | Micro cilantro-for garnish when salad is plated |

\*\*\*

| | |
|---|---|
| 4 oz. | Agave syrup |
| 1 oz. | Rice wine vinegar |
| ½ bunch | Cilantro, leaves only |
| 1 Tsp. | Salt |
| 1 Tsp. | Fish sauce |
| 1 Tsp. | Coconut Aminos |

\*\*\*\*\*\*

See notes   Almond crunchies, use on top as a garnish

**Directions:**

*Mix the dressing ingredients while you are preparing the salad ingredients by blending them on high speed in a blender for 2 minutes.*

Toss the salad ingredients in a bowl large enough to accommodate them all. Add the dressing. Toss once more plate and garnish with sprigs of micro cilantro and almond crunchies.

**Notes:**

How to make Almond crunchies; you need:

Water boiling, mix with equal amount of sugar.
2 Tbs. Salt
Oil for frying

**Directions:**

Boil water (with sugar) in a pot just large enough to hold the almonds. Heat water and dissolve the sugar, then boil almond slices for about 3 minutes. They will be tender but not break. Drain and dry off. Get oil hot. Add the almonds to crisp but not burn.

# Pad Thai Salad

Serves: 4

**Ingredients:** *(Shred salad ingredients)*

| | |
|---|---|
| ½ Cup each | Red Cabbage, Carrots, Leeks, Red Onions, Baby chiles, Scallion, Brussel sprout leaves |
| ¼ Cup | Sesame oil |
| 2 each | Jalapeño, diced |
| 3 Tbs. | Basil, shred fine |
| 3 Tbs. | Cilantro, chopped |
| ½ Cup | Bean sprouts |

\*\*\*\*\*\*

| | |
|---|---|
| ½ Cup | Peanuts, crushed |
| 3 oz. | Orange juice |
| 1 oz. | Lemon juice |
| 1 Tbs. | Fish sauce |
| 1 Tbs. | Maple syrup |
| 2 Tbs. | Cilantro, chopped |
| 2 Tbs. | Sesame oil |
| 2 Tbs. | Coconut Aminos |
| 1 ½ Cup | Rice noodles, cooked, (according to package directions) drained and tossed with 2 Tbs. Sesame oil |
| ½ Cup | Kale, baby, shred for garnish |

**Directions:**

Saute the veggies quickly in a wok on high heat 2-3 minutes to the point they just are not raw but still crisp. Cool. Make the dressing by whipping all the dressing ingredients together in a bowl. Use this to toss onto the veggies when they are cool.

Toss with the dressing ingredients. Add the herbs and jalapeno mixture. Toss in the cooked noodles. Place on separate plates with kale.

**Notes:**

To keep **Vegan** but, add protein to this dinner …. Add a ½ cup of chick peas per plate and leave out the fish sauce.

# Chick Pea Salad with Papaya dressing

Serves: 4

**Ingredients:**

| | |
|---|---|
| 1 Cup | French vinaigrette (your recipe or wishbone) |
| 5 oz. | Papaya, canned |
| 1/3 each | Papaya, ripe, fresh, save the seeds for marinades |
| 1 Tbs. | Triple sec liquor |
| As needed | Salt |
| 2 oz. | Rice wine vinegar |
| 1 oz. | Lime juice |
| .25 Cup | EVO |
| 1 Cup | Arugula, baby |
| 1 Cup | Chick peas, canned |
| ½ Cup | Red onion, jully |
| 1 Tbs. | Tarragon, chopped |
| 2 Tbs. | Scallions, cut on the bias |
| As needed | Broccoli sprouts, use as garnish |
| As needed | Pumpkin seeds, use as garnish |

**Directions:**

Mix all the dressing ingredients in a high speed blender. Grind the seeds to pebbles the size of black pepper.

Use for salad dressing.

Toss the chick peas after washing in the vinaigrette. Place on the plate decorated with Lettuces and onions. Garnish the salad with sprouts and pumpkin seeds.


## Mango and Brussel sprout salad

Serves: 4

**Ingredients:**

| | |
|---|---|
| 2 Tbs. | Lime Juice |
| 1 Tbs. | Coconut Aminos |
| 1 Tbs. | Maple syrup |
| 1 Tbs. | Garlic, crushed |
| 1 Tsp. | Ginger, chopped fine |
| ½ Cup | Peanuts, roasted ground well |
| 2 Tbs. | Baby chilies, jully |

******

| | |
|---|---|
| 1 Cup | Brussel sprouts |
| ¼ Cup | Scallions, fine jully |
| ¼ Cup | Baby chilies, jully |
| 1 Cup | Kale, baby |
| 2 each | Mango, jully, (use the from the mango cheeks) |
| ½ bunch | Cilantro leaves, torn |
| 2 Cup | Watercress |
| 1 Cup | Spinach, baby |
| 12 each | Baby chili, rings |
| ½ Cup | Peanuts, crushed |

**Directions:**

Remove the brussel sprout leaves from the heads. Mix the first part of the recipe and use for a dressing on the Brussel Sprouts.

Heat a wok very hot and brush with sesame oil. Cook the leaves for 2-3 minutes until they are not raw yet crisp. Cool toss with other salad ingredients. Dress with the top recipe.

Place spinach and watercress on a plate; add the veggie mixture on top and decorate with the pepper rings and peanuts.

# Chick Pea pancakes

Serves : 8 appetizer portions

**Ingredients:**

| | |
|---|---|
| 1 ½ Cup | Chick pea flour |
| 1 Tbs. | Rosemary, chopped fine |
| ¾ Tsp. | Salt |
| ¾ Tsp. | Black pepper |
| 1¼ Cup | Almond milk |
| 4 Tsp. | Parmesan |
| ⅓ Cup | Olive oil |
| As need | Pan spray |

**Directions:**

Mix the dry ingredients in a bowl.

In another bowl, mix the room temperature milk and cheese well. Slowly add the oil next. Stir well to make sure the grated cheese is kind of melted into the milk.

Add into the dry mix and stir well again.

Heat a skillet to medium heat.

Pour the batter into the pan. Warm the cakes slowly. If the pan is too hot the Parmesan cheese burns.

Cook very slow. Flip over when the batter seems to be dry enough to have a sturdy crust....that helps the cake stay together.

Plate like picture below....

*Sweet Potato Cakes, recipe follows*

# Sweet Potato Cakes

*Notes two part Recipe...make separately. This will become one of your favorite side dishes or light lunch recipe.*

Serves: 4

**Ingredients:**

### *Sauce:*

| | |
|---|---|
| 1/2 Cup | Cashew yogurt (or plant based yogurt) |
| 1 Tbs. | EVO |
| 1 Tbs. | Lemon juice |
| 1 Tbs. | Dill, chopped fresh |
| 1 Tbs. | Capers, chopped |
| As needed | Seasalt |

### *Second part:*

| | |
|---|---|
| 2 each | Sweet potatoes, peeled and cut into chunks |
| 1 each | Shallots, fine dice |
| 1 each | Chili, red, fine chopped |
| 1 each | Apple - honey Crisp, finely chopped |
| 1/3 Cup | Cornstarch |
| As needed | Coconut oil, enough to fry in a pan |

**Directions:**

**To make the sauce:**

Mix all the first part of the recipe. Let chill in the refrigerator while you are making the rest of the recipe.

**To make the Cakes:** Boil potatoes till they are soft. Drain and let rest in the strainer for all the liquids to be removed; mash the potatoes quickly and don't mash too long. *Just roughly smashed.*

Add the pancakes ingredients, Cornstarch (*might need more because of the moisture of the mixture*) and seasonings then separate this batch into equal portions- so they can be formed into cakes.

Heat the oil, cook the cakes to golden and they hold their shape. Don't flip until they are slightly brown. You can look at the edges of the cakes to see if they are the right color.

Flip only once and let the other side brown.

Drain on paper towels after you remove them.

**To Serve:**

Set atop Spinach, Arugula and goat cheese dressed with a little of your favorite balsamic vinaigrette. Place a dollop of the yogurt sauce on top the cakes when ready to eat.

# Arugula Apple, Pineapple and Blueberry Salad

Serving: 4

**Ingredient:**

| | |
|---|---|
| 4 Cups | Arugula, baby, torn |
| ¼ each | Pineapple, fresh, peeled, cored, and chopped |
| ½ each | Apple, Fuji (a sweet apple) |
| ½ Pint | Blueberries, fresh |
| ¼ each | Onion, red, thinly sliced |
| 3 Tbs. | Goat cheese, crumbled |
| ¼ Cup | Cilantro, chopped |
| 3 Tbs. | Lemon juice |
| 1 Tbs. | EVO olive oil |
| 2 Tsp. | Maple syrup |
| ¼ Tsp. | Seasalt |

**Directions:**

A great summer dish for an entrée or a side dish. Mix arugula, fruit, red onion, Goat's cheese and cilantro in a salad bowl. Whisk lemon juice, olive oil, maple syrup and salt in a small bowl; pour dressing over salad and toss everything well. Use in place of the veggies that most people expect on the plate.

# Grits with Kale, Avocado and Black Bean Salad

Serves: 4

*Research has shown that Kale's carotenoids can act as antioxidants. They help stop free radicals from damaging DNA that can lead to cancer. The vitamin C in kale is also a powerful antioxidant. Kale is one of the most nutritious greens— and one of the easiest to grow in your garden. Rich in vitamins A, K, and C, with red, purple and black varieties containing nearly double the antioxidants of green kale.*

**Ingredients:**

| | |
|---|---|
| 1 recipe | GF Polenta, see recipe above |
| 3 Tbs. | Lime juice |
| 1 Tbs. | Dijon mustard |
| 1 Tbs. | Jalapeño pepper, finely diced (seeds removed) |
| 1 Tsp. | Honey |
| ½ Tsp. | Cumin, ground |
| ¼ Tsp. | Coriander, ground |
| to taste | Sea salt |

### *Salad:*

| | |
|---|---|
| 1 bunch | Tuscan (*black*) Kale, (*see notes*) ribs removed and leaves, thinly sliced |
| 1 (14 ounce) | Black beans, rinsed and drained well |
| 1 each | Avocado, diced |
| 1 each | Tomato, diced |
| ½ Cup | Sheep's milk feta cheese (*imported*), crumbled |
| ⅓ Cup | Peanuts, shelled |
| 1 Tsp. | Sugar |
| ⅛ Tsp. | Seasalt |
| ½ Cup | Cilantro, chopped |

**Directions:**

Make the corn fritter recipe (*Grits*) from the recipe on page 124. Flow the recipe steps and place on a large entrée plate. Cool and add a little of with the second part of the recipe.

Whisk olive oil with the rest of the dressing ingredients. Whisk rapidly with a wire whisk until the dressing is smooth and combined completely.

Next place sliced kale in a bowl and sprinkle sea salt over kale. Massage salt into the kale until leaves are darker (in color) and fragrant. Drizzle enough dressing over kale to lightly coat. Toss well.

Now fold in black beans, avocado, and feta cheese. Let this rest for 5 minutes.

Place peanuts into a skillet and sprinkle sugar and 1/8 teaspoon salt over peanuts; cook and stir over medium-low heat until fragrant and sugar is dissolved, 3 to 5 minutes. Cool peanuts and chop.

Distribute salad among serving plates and then top with toasted pecans and cilantro.

### *Option:*
*Drizzle plates with EVO for additional richness.*

### Notes:

*Not all **Feta** cheese is the same. Domestically produced cheese is made with Cow's milk. Real imported Feta is made with Sheep's milk. Which is so much better for you when it comes to healthy eating.*

### *Tuscan Kale:*

*Mature curly kale has a peppery flavor with a pleasantly bitter edge. Lacinato (Tuscan) kale tastes less bitter, it is more tender and its flavor can be described as earthy, yet delicate, with a hint of nutty sweetness. When looking for a great Fall recipe, this is the perfect time to cook with kale because cooler weather makes Kale taste sweeter.*

# Avalanche of Kale and Quinoa

Serves: 6

**Ingredients:**

| | |
|---|---|
| 2 Cups | Water |
| 2 Tbs. | Yellow curry powder |
| 2 Tbs. | Kosher salt |
| 1 Cup | Quinoa |
| 10 each | Kale leaves, cut into small pieces |
| 3 Tbs. | EVO olive oil |
| 2 Tbs. | Lemon juice |
| 1 Tsp. | Dijon mustard |
| 1 large | Garlic clove, minced |
| 1 Tsp. | Black pepper, cracked |
| ½ Tsp. | Sea salt |
| 1 Cup | Pecans, chopped up |
| 1 Cup | Beets, cooked soft, diced large |
| 1 Cup | Currants |
| ½ Cup | Grapes, green |
| ¾ Cup | Goat's cheese, crumbled |

**Directions:**

Bring water to a boil in a saucepan with salt and curry. Stir quinoa into the boiling water, reduce heat to medium-low, place cover on the saucepan, and cook until water absorbs into the quinoa, about 15 minutes. Remove saucepan from heat and let rest covered for 5 minutes. Remove cover and allow quinoa to cool completely.

Put kale in a large mixing bowl.

In a separate bowl whisk together lemon juice, Dijon mustard, garlic, pepper, salt and finally the olive oil, together until the oil emulsifies into the mixture. Drizzle over kale. Add cooled quinoa, pecans, beets, currants, grapes and goat's cheese to the dressed kale and toss to incorporate everything.

# Corn Flour dusted Corn Fritters

**Ingredients:**

| | |
|---|---|
| ⅓ Cup | Cornmeal |
| ⅓ Cup | GF flour |
| ½ Tsp. | Baking powder |
| Pinch | Kosher salt and freshly ground pepper |
| ⅓ Cup | Almond milk, well-shaken |
| 1 large | Egg substitute |
| 2 Tbs. | Vegan Butter |
| 2 each | Shallot, finely chopped |
| 3 each | Green onions, whites, thinly sliced |
| 1 ½ Cups | Corn kernels |
| 2 Tbs. | Canola oil, for frying |

**Directions:**

Preheat your oven to 375 degrees. Mix the dry ingredients together. Add the butter and mix to make the batter crumbly. Add the almond milk. Add the corn and the onions.

Place the batter on a baking pan that has been oiled. Cook in the oven for 15 minutes. Cool and let rest 10 minutes before pulling out of the pan and cutting it into 6 equal pieces.

*To serve:*

Warm oil in a skillet and place the fritters in the oil to warm only to the point of not being cold. Serve with sauce. (see marinara sauce in the other recipes).

*Previous recipe...Corn fritters with GF Marinara*

# Veggie Quinoa Bites

Tired of the same old snacks? Try something new with these vegetable quinoa bites! Packed with protein and they are portable. They are great for on the go families.

Serves: 6

**Ingredients:**

| | |
|---|---|
| 1 Cup | Quinoa, use the tricolored variety |
| 1 ½ Cups | Veggie stock, see notes from above recipe |
| ¼ Tsp. | Sea salt |
| 1 medium | Zucchini, grated, let drain in a strainer |
| 1 medium | Carrot, grated, let drain in a strainer |
| 1/3 lb. | Cheddar cheese, shredded |
| ¼ bunch | Italian parsley, minced |
| 4 large | Eggs, organic |
| ¾ Cup | Gluten-free flour |

**Directions:**

Preheat oven to 350F. Prepare quinoa by placing in a small saucepan with veggie stock and a ¼ Tsp. salt.

Bring to a simmer, cover, and reduce heat to low. Continue to cook for 15 minutes or until liquid has been absorbed. Turn off heat and allow to cool.

In a medium mixing bowl, combine the remaining ingredients with cooled quinoa. Scoop mixture with a #40-scoop (around an ounce) and place on two parchment lined baking pans.

Bake at 350F for 15-20 minutes. Cool and wrap it you like to keep them for a picnic or in-office snack.

*Cauliflower, Buffalo style  - **next recipe***

# Cauliflower, Buffalo style

4 servings

**Ingredients:**

| | |
|---|---|
| ¾ Cup | GF flour |
| 1 Tsp. | Paprika |
| 2 Tsp. | Garlic powder |
| 1 Tsp. | Seasalt |
| ½ Tsp. | Pepper |
| 1 head | Cauliflower, break up into large pieces |
| 3 Cup | Almond milk (cooked to reduce volume to 3/4 cup) |
| ¼ Cup | Hot sauce, (or Sriracha sauce) |
| 2 Tbs. | Coconut oil |
| 1 Tbs. | Agave |

**Directions:**

Preheat the oven to 450°F (230°C).

Have water boiling in a pot big enough to cook the cauliflower. Line a baking sheet with parchment paper.

In a large bowl, add the flour, paprika, garlic powder, salt, pepper, and stir until well-combined.

Break the head of cauliflower into florets, about 1½-inches wide.

Blanch the cauliflower in the boiling water for 5 minutes. Remove drain well then, place in flour mixture....making sure each piece is evenly coated, shake off excess flour. Arrange the coated cauliflower on the baking sheet.

Make a batter with liquids in the recipe. (Make extra by doubling the liquids in the recipe...if you want to use as a dip) Toss the flour-coated cauliflower in to the liquid batter. Scoop out with a slotted spoon on to the parchment-lined baking sheet.

Bake in the 450-degree oven for 20 minutes, flipping halfway through the time to make sure they evenly cooked.

Serve with more sauce if you like. Use the Avocado butter on page 147 ... to melt over the top if you like.

# Pan-seared Scallops with pickled veggie

Serves 4

## Ingredients:

| | |
|---|---|
| 4 Tsp. | Avocado oil (buttery) spread, *Pure Blends* |
| Pinch | Seasons, (each....garlic granulated, onion powder, white pepper, sea salt, paprika-mixed together) |
| 8 each | Scallop (U-10 size), remove the side muscle, seasoned |
| 1 bunch | Asparagus, medium size, blanch in boiling water and then shock (dipping *in ice water*) |
| 1/3 Cup | Veggies, julienne sliced, (equal amounts of Bell peppers, Red Onions, Carrots, Celery, Leeks) |
| 1/3 Cup | Sun Sprouts, leaves pulled from stems |
| ¼ Cup | Arugula, baby |
| 1 Cup | Spinach, baby |
| ½ Cup | Microgreens (Arugula, Basil, Cilantro) use as you like for garnishing |
| As needed | Plate sauce, see recipe below, see picture for an artistic approach |
| As needed | Leaf dressing, see recipe to follow |
| As needed | Pickled veggies, see recipes to follow |

**Directions:**

Complete the separate recipes. Plate the recipes in sequence building one recipe atop another. Let the seasoned scallops rest on a plate while you are heating a sauté pan and finishing the sub-recipes.

- Plate the decorative sauce on the service plate.

- Top the sauce with salad.

- Top salad with the pickled veggies and cold-blanched asparagus.

- Top with the seared scallops. Garnish the entire plate with micro-greens.

**Plate sauce recipe:**

| | |
|---|---|
| ½ each | Avocado (about 1 Lb.), use the Caribbean, shelled, meat only |
| 2 each | Key Limes, juiced, use fresh for best results |
| 3 Tbs. | E.V.O. |
| As needed | Salt and white pepper |

**To Make the recipe:**  In a steel bowl, chunk up the avocado and then smash up with a fork. Add the lime juice and Season. Add the oil and mix smooth by mixing in a food processor - to completely smooth to sauce consistency. Use more oil to make smoother if you are using larger avocados. Use this for decorating your serving plate without covering the entire base, just smear decoratively with the black end of a serving spoon.

**Salad Leaf dressing recipe:**

| | |
|---|---|
| 2 Tbs. | Lemon juice |
| ½ Tsp. | Dijon mustard |

1 Cup         EVO
Pinch          Seasalt and white pepper

***To make:*** using a whisk and a metal bowl, whisk the first two ingredients together. Slowly add the EVO oil. As you whip together the dressing - it combines to become thickened. Season with the salt and pepper. Add the dressing to the leaves to glaze slightly and place the salad on the plate above the sauce (recipe below), as you see in the picture above.

### ***Pickled veggies recipe:***

½ Tsp.      (*of each*) Mustard seeds and Coriander seeds, *first toast in a dry skillet to boost their potency*
½ Cup      Red wine vinegar
¼ Tsp.      (*of each*) Salt, powder ginger and red pepper flakes
4 each      Bay leaf
½ Cup      Ice, cubes or flaked

### **Directions:**

*The Day before* Heat a skillet on high heat. Leaving completely dry, toast the whole seed spices to make them more fragrant. Toss in the pan for about 3 minutes. Then add the vinegar and heat the vinegar with all the spices on medium heat for 10 minutes. Remove from heat and cool. Add ice to completely cool and to thin the vinegar content.

Place the julienned veggies in the pickling solution (in a non-reactive bowl), leave overnight, drain veggies to use in this plate.

### ***Other steps:***

Blanch the asparagus and then place it in a bowl of water overfilled with ice. As soon as the asparagus is removed from the water dip into the ice water. This is called shocking the veggies and this process stops the cooking cycle and sets the color of the asparagus so they remain vibrant in color (....*they won't change in color unless you keep these for a long time in the refrigerator*).

- *Slice a few of the asparagus on a severe bias for decoration on the plate as shown in the picture.*

Heat a sauté pan. Sear the seasoned scallops over high heat with the avocado oil spread, until they are seared to medium-rare (*Cook about 1 ½ minutes on each side for U-10 sized scallops*). Take the seared scallops and place them on a warm holding plate until you are ready to finish the serving plates with other recipes.

- The scallops will release juices on to this plate and not over the presentation plate.

Follow the picture to use as a guide to layer all the recipes to finish the plate.

**Notes**:

Make the recipe for the pickling liquid a day ahead and macerate the ingredients for at least a day. You can make more veggies and leave in the refrigerator and eat later with other recipes.

- To make something special for the summertime picnics you will be attending this year....

- Make a double batch of the pickling liquid.

- Take a watermelon and wash the skin well. Cut the husk from the watermelon's red flesh (using for watermelon salad in a bowl with fried chicken of course).

- Take the green and white husk and place them on a rotary slicer (deli meat slicer).

- Slice across the husk so you get the green outer skin, the white inner layer, and a little pink color with each slice.

- Soak these slices in this recipe's veggie brine and, refrigerate for up to a week ahead of the time before you want to use them.

- Remove from brine. Drizzle with a couple of tablespoons of Orange Blossom Honey. Toss well and serve.

- Serve (as a side salad) with grilled foods and fried chicken or your picnic.

*Pan-seared Scallops with pickled veggie salad*

*Veggie forward GF Light lunch*

# Light Farro Nosh

Serves: 6

**Ingredient**

| | |
|---|---|
| 1 Tbs. | EVO olive oil |
| 2 cloves | Garlic, minced |
| 2 Tsp. | Lemon juice |
| To taste | Salt and ground black pepper |
| 2 Cups | Veggie broth |
| 1 Cup | Farro, an Ancient grain |
| 2 Cups | Kale, chopped |
| ½ Cup | Goat's milk crumbled cheese |

**Directions:**

Mix olive oil, garlic, lemon juice, salt, and pepper together in a bowl.

In a heavy bottom skillet or a Wok, heat for two or three minutes and add the Farro grain. Toss well and continue to move the grain around the skillet while they toast. Combine veggie broth and Farro together in a large frying pan or wok; bring to a boil. Reduce heat to medium and simmer until Farro is tender and the broth is absorbed, 20 to 25 minutes.

Stir olive oil mixture into Farro until Farro is coated. Add kale to Farro mixture; cook and stir until kale is wilted, 2 to 3 minutes. Sprinkle feta cheese over Farro salad and stir until cheese is incorporated. Season salad with more salt and pepper if desired.

# Hearty Yam and White Bean Hash

Serves: 4

**Ingredients:**

| | |
|---|---|
| 1 Tbs. | EVO olive oil |
| 1 each | Russet potato, diced |
| 1 each | Sweet Yam, diced |
| 2 each | Garlic, minced |
| 1 each | Yellow onion, diced |
| ½ each | Green Bell pepper, diced |
| 1 Cup | Collard greens, de-stemmed, sliced into thin ribbons |
| 2 Cups | White beans, cooked |
| 1 Tsp. | Cumin |
| 1 Tsp. | Paprika, smoked |
| 1/2 Tsp. | Thyme, dried |
| 2 each | Green onions, chopped |
| To taste | Sea salt and black pepper |
| 1 Tbs. | **Za'atar**, (see next recipe) |

**Directions:**

Add the olive oil to a large pan over medium heat. Add the potatoes and yams and cook for 8-10 minutes, flipping occasionally until the potatoes are browning and getting crisp.

Add the garlic, onions, bell peppers, and collard greens and cook for about 5 minutes, until the onions are translucent and the bell peppers are softening.

Add the beans, cumin, paprika, thyme, and green onions and cook for an additional 5 minutes, until beans are heated thoroughly. Season with Za'atar, salt and pepper to taste and serve hot.

## Za'atar Spice Blend:

**Ingredients:**

| | |
|---|---|
| 1 Tbs. | Pan-roasted sesame seeds |
| ¼ Cup | Sumac, ground |
| 2 Tbs. | Thyme, dried |
| 2 Tbs. | Marjoram, dried |
| 2 Tbs. | Oregano, dried |
| 1 Tsp. | Seasalt |

**Directions:**

Roast the seeds separately in a hot skillet, until brown. Remove from heat and cool. Grind them in a coffee grinder. Add to the rest of the flavorings.

Use as a topping for other foods like Hummus.

.

## GF Polenta with Caramelized Onions, Mushrooms and Marinara, *see notes*

Serves: 4

*This recipe has adjoining recipes. Follow the directions per recipe and THEN, compile them all into one dish. Make the marinara sauce use it on the bottom of each plate. You will have extra sauce for dipping or other recipes. Then run a ladle though the sauce to spread it across the plate.*

*Scoop out the cooked polenta in the center of the (sauced) plate topping it with the mushrooms and the caramelized onions in recipe on page 137.*

*See the Grits recipe seen previously in this book to make this polenta recipe into a salad entrée.*

## Ingredients:

| | |
|---|---|
| 3 Tbs. | EVO oil |
| ½ Cup | Onions, diced finely |
| 1 Cup | Corn Polenta (white, Ground grits) |
| 2 Cups | Veggie stock |
| ½ Cup | Avocado butter |
| ⅓ Cup | Parmesan cheese |
| 1 Tsp. | Seasalt |
| ½ Tsp. | Cumin |
| 1 Tsp. | Thyme, chopped |
| 1 recipe | Onions, *use Vegan recipe page 161* |
| 3 Tbs. | EVO |
| 1 Cup | Mushrooms, button (see notes) |
| 1 Tsp. | Balsamic vinegar |

## Directions:

Heat the oil and sauté the onions soft, about 3 minutes. Add the corn and with a wooden spoon stir all well together. Continue to stir for 3 more minutes. It should look a little different after cooking the cornmeal with the onions. Add the veggie stock. *If you make your own stock use more onions than you would for your usual Mirepoix laced stock.*

Cook and continue to stir all the while as the cornmeal absorbs the stock and becomes thicker. Lower the heat and continue to stir while cooking about 20 minutes. The polenta is ready when the meal is soft and look like a pudding.

Add in the cheese and seasonings. Stir well to incorporate.

Heat the EVO in a skillet. After it gets smoking hot, add the mushrooms to cook. Stir-fry the mushrooms for 3 to 5 minutes. Season the mushrooms by sprinkling with balsamic vinegar. Remove from the pan and top the polenta after it is plated atop the sauce.

*Notes:*

*Because it is rich in fiber; **corn** also helps lower cholesterol levels and minimizes colon cancer risk. Corn may help minimize the risk of lung cancer and helps promote healthy lungs.*

*White button **mushrooms** have been shown in studies to suppress aromatase activity and estrogen biosynthesis, in addition to inhibiting proliferation of estrogen receptor positive breast cancer cells. They have been proven to have the most powerful breast cancer chemo-preventive properties.*

# GF Marinara sauce

Serves: 8-10

*Of course Tomatoes are full of Lycopene. (see notes that follows). It is another reason everyone loves Marinara sauce.*

**Ingredients:**

| | |
|---|---|
| 2 Tbs. | EVO oil |
| 1 Each | Onion, yellow, diced |
| 2 each | Garlic cloves, fine diced |
| 2 (28oz.) | Tomatoes, imported, Plum (canned for convenience) |
| 1 bunch | Basil, chopped roughly |
| 1 Tbs. | Thyme, chopped fine |
| To taste | Seasalt, as needed to balance taste |
| Pinch | Sugar, as needed to balance taste |

**Directions:**

Heat oil. Sauté the onions then the garlic. Cook about 7 minutes.

Add the herbs and cook another 3 minutes. Add the tomatoes crushing them up by hand.

Lower the heat and cook for 15 minutes. Then take an immersion blender and place it in to the sauce. Grind the sauce up well.

Keep warm.

Serve on the bottom of the plate, place the polenta (see recipe on previous page) on top with the caramelized onions onto the top as a garnish.

### NOTES:

Why is lycopene good?

Lycopene has been linked to health benefits ranging from heart health[19] to protection against sunburns and certain types of cancers. Lycopene is a plant nutrient with antioxidant properties.

# Vegan Bolognese ~ Italian gravy

*Sunday Gravy is an Italian family's name for what the rest of us call spaghetti sauce. It is the most well-known of all Sunday meal sauces but this Italian sauce is now one that is Vegan in nature. It is Hearty - Protein-packed - Vegetable forward and delicious and can be a stock recipe in your repertoire for weekly healthy dining choices.*

**Ingredients:**

| | |
|---|---|
| 2 oz. | EVO olive oil |
| 1 each | Shallot (minced) |
| 1 small | Yellow onion, fine chopped |
| 4 cloves | Garlic (minced) |
| 2-3 each | Carrots (finely shredded, then chopped fine) |
| 1 pinch | Sea salt |
| 1 each | Tomato sauce, canned, *your favorite brand* |
| 1 pinch | Red pepper flake |
| 2 Tsp. | Basil, dried |

---

19    https://www.ncbi.nlm.nih.gov/pmc/articles/PMC3850026/

| | |
|---|---|
| 1 Tsp. | Oregano, dried |
| 1 Tsp. | Coconut sugar |
| ½ Cup | Water (to thin out if you want) |
| ¾ Cup | Red lentils (rinsed and drained) |

**Directions:**

Heat a large rimmed skillet over medium heat. Once hot, add EVO, shallot, and garlic. Add the onion and sauté for 10 minutes. Stir frequently, until slightly soft. Turn down heat if starting to brown. I like to use extra oil here that will make the sauce richer in taste overall.

Add carrots and a pinch of salt and stir. Cook for 3-4 minutes more, then add marinara sauce and stir to coat.

Add red pepper flake, basil, oregano, coconut sugar, water, and lentils. Increase heat slightly and bring mixture to a simmer, then reduce heat to low/medium-low and continue cooking until lentils are tender – stir– about 17-20 minutes. Add a bit more water if the mixture gets too thick.

Once the lentils are cooked, taste and adjust seasonings as needed, adding more salt to taste, coconut sugar for sweetness, red pepper flake for heat, or herbs for flavor balance.

# Asian-style Braised Pork (Slow cooker recipe)

Serves: 4-6 people

This is the recipe you need to serve with rice or veggies in the following pages.

**Ingredients:**

| | |
|---|---|
| 3 lbs. | Pork shoulder or Pork butt |
| 2 lbs. | Carrots, chopped |
| 1 lb. | Leeks, chopped |
| 1 lb. | Celery, chopped |
| 1/3 Cup | Coconut Aminos |
| 1/4 Cup | Honey |
| 2 Tbs. | Brown sugar |
| 1 Tbs. | Sesame oil |
| 1 Tbs. | Rice wine vinegar |
| 1 Tbs. | Hoisin sauce |
| 4-5 each | Garlic, smashed |
| 10 oz. | Mirin, (sweetened sake) |

**Directions:**

Optional: Remove fat from the pork shoulders or pork butt. Add the veggies to the bottom of the slow cooker. Mix the rest of the ingredients in a small bowl and then rub the meat with this mixture. Place the meat on top of the veggies. Add the Mirin and let cook covered and check occasionally to turn the meat every hour or so.

Cover and cook on the high setting of the slow cooker. Cook till tender for about 4 hours. When done remove the pork and place it on a large platter.

Then use a fork to shred the pork (it should come apart easily). Serve with rice and veggies from the pot.

# Asian-Style Braised Salmon

Serves: 6 people

*Served in a way that makes a great family style dinner. Using an old-fashion Dutch oven this recipe is one of a kind.*

## Ingredients:

| | |
|---|---|
| To taste | EVO olive oil |
| 1 - 3 lb. | Salmon fillet, entire side of the fish |
| To taste | Seasalt |
| 5 each | Garlic, smashed and finely chopped |
| One | Ginger, 2-inch piece, peeled and grated |
| 4 oz. | Coconut Aminos |
| 2 oz. | Rice wine vinegar |
| 2 oz. | Oyster sauce |
| 2 Tbs. | Maple syrup |
| 2 Tsp. | Sambal Oelek |
| 1 each | Star anise, ground fine |
| 3 Cups | Chicken stock |
| 1 each | Orange, zest and juice, zest removed in wide strips with a peeler |

## Directions:

Take the Dutch oven and get it ready for use with the whole fillet of fish. Preheat an oven to 400 degrees.

Oil down the salmon and season (liberally) the salmon fillet with seasalt. Let rest on a tray while you are making the glaze portion of the recipe. Paint on the glaze to the salmon fillet.

When glazed well, place the glazed fillet in the Dutch oven and add the chicken stock carefully not to wash over the fillets.

Warm the Dutch oven on top of an open flame for about 2 minutes. Close the lid and place into your preheated oven. Cook for 15 minutes covered. For larger thick fillets that are more than 2 inches thick cook another 5 minutes.

Remove the cover of the pan and look to see if the fillet is whitish and firm to the touch.

If you use a thermometer cook until the fillets are 140 degrees in the thickest portion of the fillet.

Carefully remove the fillet to a large platter using 2 large metal spatulas so the fillet won't break apart. Place on the platter and leave in a warm spot on top of the oven.

Take the Dutch oven and place the pan back on top of an open flame and cook the juices in the bottom of the pan over a high heat. Stirring rapidly - the entire time; cook to reduce the volume of the juices to a glaze. Place the glaze in a gravy boat to be used as an accompaniment for the fillets. When the fillet is on the platter cut into portions for each person at the table.

Serve with the Kimchee recipe that follows using it as a veggie in a decorative manner.

### *To make the glaze:*

In a saucepan place the garlic and ginger in a shallow pan and add the soy and the next 5 ingredients. Let simmer for five minutes. Stir well the entire time. Use this glaze for coating the fillets (before placing the fillets in the Dutch oven) by painting it on the fillets with a brush. Coat well don't worry if it seems light. The flavors are bold.

### *Notes:*

Use the **Pineapple Kimchee** (*next recipe*) listed below as a side dish that pairs perfectly for your dinner.

# Pineapple Kimchee

Serves: 12-15 (side dish salads)

**Ingredients:**

| | |
|---|---|
| 2.5 lbs. | Cabbage, shreded |
| 3 each | Mango, green, julienne |
| 3 each | Red onion, julienne |
| 1 each | Red bell pepper, julienne |
| 2 oz. | Ginger, pickled |
| 2 oz. | Carrot, julienne |
| 2 each | Pineapple, under ripe, julienne |
| ½ Cup | Kosher salt |
| 2 oz. | Sriracha sauce |
| 1 oz. | Sesame oil |
| 2 bunch | Cilantro, chopped |

**Directions:**

Cut the veggies in sequence. Layering each with a portion of the salt and sriracha sauce. Add the mangoes, pineapple and ginger toss well. Add the sesame oil and cilantro. Refrigerate for up to a week. Drain before using.

***Notes:***

I have used unripe green papaya in place of the cabbage that makes new salad and a more Asian twist for the recipe. Use for Pork and Seafood.

# Mediterranean Pasta with Arugula, Tomato and Sheep's Milk Feta

Serves: 4

## Ingredients:

| | |
|---|---|
| 8 oz. | Orecchiette pasta |
| 3 Cups | Arugula, chopped fresh |
| ½ each | English cucumber |
| 1 Cup | Tomato, diced |
| 1 each | Avocado, cut up into bite size pieces |
| ½ Cup | Feta, white Sheep's milk cheese |
| 2-3 Tbs. | Parsley, chopped |

## Second recipe dressing:

| | |
|---|---|
| ¼ Cup | Avocado oil |
| ¼ Cup | Key Lime juice (5-6 limes) |
| ¼ Tsp. | Lime zest |
| 2 Tbs. | Dijon mustard |
| 2 each | Shallots, freshly. minced |
| ¼ Tsp. | Oregano, dried |
| ¼ Tsp. | Seasalt and red pepper flakes |

## Directions:

First let's make the dressing. Zest 1 lime and set aside. Juice your limes to yield 1/4 cup of juice and add to a small/medium mason jar. Add the zest and remaining dressing ingredients and close the lid tightly. Shake to emulsify the dressing. It will stay in emulsion for a few minutes.

Next cook pasta for about 9 minutes. Chop arugula, cucumber, tomato and parsley and add to a large bowl. Save the avocado for just before serving. Once your pasta is perfectly al dente, strain in a colander and run cold water to halt the cooking process and chill the pasta slightly. Then add the drained pasta to your veggies and toss together.

Shake once more if needed and add to the salad. Toss well to coat. Lastly add avocado and feta on top and gently fold into the salad. Add salt and pepper.

## Chicken Swawama

This recipe makes oven-roasted chicken thighs a fantastic picnic lunch or leftover cold salad.

Serves: 6 to 8

**Ingredients:**

| | |
|---|---|
| ½ Cup | Olive oil |
| 2 Tbs. | Cumin, granular |
| 2 Tbs. | Paprika, smoked |
| 1 Tsp. | Allspice, granular |
| 2 Tbs. | Turmeric, granular |
| 1 Tbs. | Garlic, granular |
| ½ Tbs. | Cinnamon, granular |
| ½ Tbs. | Cayenne pepper, ground |
| 1 Tsp. | Seasalt |
| 2 Lbs. | Chicken Thighs |

**Directions:**

Remove any skin from chicken thighs. Then mix the spices into the oil. Add the oil to the chicken thighs and let marinate at least three hours. Then grill or roast until done.

- You can serve this over top any salad recipe in this book.

- Or can use this as the protein content in a pita pocket.

# Avocado *Herbed* Butter

**Ingredients:**

| | |
|---|---|
| 6 Tbs. | Avocado butter, softened |
| ½ Tsp. | Cumin (ground to a powder) |
| ¼ Tsp. | Cilantro leaves, dried |
| ¼ Tsp. | Basil, dried |
| Pinch | Sea salt |
| Pinch | Red chili flakes |

**Directions:**

In a small bowl combine (use a hand whip or mixing machine) the room-temperature softened butter, cumin, cilantro and basil, salt and crushed red pepper. Stir until well mixed. Chill and scoop atop food.

*Or...*

Another way you can use this is to double the recipe then scrape out onto a 12x14 inch wax paper. Fold over the paper to make a log out of the paper. Roll out the log to make it rounded. Twist the ends up to close the roll. Freeze the roll for a few hours or overnight.

Remove the paper and slice this roll of butter into coins. Place the coins over the hot grilled food. Let the coins melt as you walk the dishes to your table and serve.

*<u>Use for:</u>*

Atop **grilled chicken** and **seafood fillets**. Use on top toast or baked casseroles for a savory glaze.

Or, use it for other recipes like a buttery topping on baked sweet potatoes, pan-roasted baby potatoes and roasted squash and pumpkin dishes.

Quinoa Superbowl

# Quinoa Superbowl

Serves: 4

*Break recipe up into stages....it makes it easier to prepare closer to the time of service and being prepared ahead of time like this gives you the ability to change ingredients on the fly.... so, you can replace and switch items that are more seasonally available.*

## **Recipe Overview:**

(*toss when ready with the rest of the recipe stages*)

## **Ingredients:**

| | |
|---|---|
| 2 Cups | Quinoa (precooked with curry spice) cool |
| ½ Cup | Baby Spinach |
| ⅓ Cup | Baby Arugula |
| ⅓ Cup | Baby Kale (only use baby, not chopped full-grown kale) |
| 15 each | Cherry / Grape tomatoes, halved |
| 1 each | Cucumber wedges, chopped roughly |
| ½ each | Caribbean avocado, (see note), chopped roughly |
| ¼ Cup | Radish, sliced thin |
| ⅓ Cup | Herbs like: parsley, chives, tarragon, dill ...up to you. |
| ¼ Cup | Microgreens, Cilantro (*garnish the final plate*) --See notes |
| 4 oz. to order | Boniato, skin on, sliced thin, (see notes) dry, cooked |
| ½ Cup | Onions, red, julienne (optional) |
| ½ Cup | Fennel, shaved thinly (optional) |
| ½ Cup | Pineapple, grilled thick slices and roughly chopped **(optional)** |
| ¼ Cup | Feta cheese (optional) |
| ½ Cup | Red Bell pepper, roasted (optional) |

## ***Dressing:***

| | |
|---|---|
| ½ Cup | Red bell pepper, roasted, dice |
| ½ Cup | Shallots, diced |
| 4 each | Jalapeño peeled, chopped |
| 2 oz. | Red wine vinegar |
| 4 oz. | Sherry vinegar |

| | |
|---|---|
| 2 oz. | Coconut Aminos |
| 2 Tsp. | Dijon mustard |
| 2 oz. | Orange juice concentrate |
| 2 oz. | Apple juice concentrate |
| 1.5 Cups | EVO olive oil |
| Dash | Sea Salt, as needed |

## Directions:

First, cook the quinoa in twice as much salted water as the volume of quinoa … Adding three heaping tablespoons of curry powder to the water. Cook until quinoa "pops" and becomes tender. About 20 minutes for me usually. Dry by draining in a colander if necessary.

Toss with the dressing and the other items in the top half of the recipe as close to service as possible. Place on plates as shown in the picture above.

### *For the dressing:*

Process the shallots and the peppers in a food processor until smooth. Add the liquids. Let incorporate well. Add sweetener and add oil slowly making a thickened vinaigrette. Season with salt.

*(Toss the veggie half of the recipe with dressing. Add this to the cooked quinoa just before you serve the salad.)*

### *Notes:*

Avocados from Florida or the Caribbean are not as fatty as the Mexican Haas avocado, but both are delicious and nutritious. Our advice is to go with what you prefer.

Boniato…. when you use this Caribbean sweet potato, wash the skins well and place in a bowl of water. Let them soak for up to 6 hours, then drain in a coriander and pat them dry before using. Cook the potatoes in hot oil until slightly brown, as shown in the photograph.

### _Microgreens:_

_Tiny **Microgreens** packed with Nutrients._

- They may be tiny, but a new study shows trendy microgreens punch well above their weight when it comes to nutrition.

Researchers found microgreens like red cabbage, cilantro, and radish contain up to **40 times** higher levels of vital nutrients than their mature counterparts. Microgreens in general are superior in nutritional value than the mature plants. Researchers say they were astonished by the results.

Microgreens are young seedlings of edible vegetables and herbs harvested less than 14 days after germination. They are usually about 1-3 inches long and come in a rainbow of colors, which has made them popular in recent years as garnishes.

### _Microgreens Pack Nutritional Punch:_

Researchers evaluated levels of four groups of vital nutrients, including vitamin K, vitamin C, vitamin E, Lutein, and beta-carotene, in 25 different commercially grown microgreens.

Vitamin C, vitamin K, and vitamin E levels were highest among red Cabbage, garnet Amaranth, and green Daikon radish Microgreens. "They found that the levels were not only detectable but in some cases **4-6 times more** concentrated than in the leaves of a mature plant."

Because Microgreens are harvested right after germination, all the nutrients they need to grow are there, If they are harvested at the right time they are very concentrated with nutrients, and the flavor and texture is also good.

# 10 Hour roasted Pork

Serves: 8

*When you have a big group of friends coming over to celebrate a holiday, this recipe is your go-to. Not only is the pork roast better for your pocket book (costing less than $2.50 a pound) and is healthier than the beef roast we all have used in the past. This is one of those multi-step yet, easy to accomplish recipes once you realize everything is made ahead of time. You'll need a large crock pot and Dutch oven because of the size of the roast. This a great recipe to use large "Charger-size plates".*

## *Main recipe:*

**Ingredients:**

| | |
|---|---|
| 5 to 6 lbs. | Pork Shoulder roast |
| 1 Tsp. | Pre-seasoning – of each (garlic-granular, onion powder, black pepper, Sea salt) |
| 4 Tbs. | Olive oil |
| 1 lb. | Onion, roughly chopped |
| 1 lb. | Cippolini Onions, peeled use whole |
| ½ Cup | Garlic, peeled, whole kernels |
| 2 dozen | Red Potatoes, small size |
| 1 head | Celery, roughly cut, save the leaves for garnish |
| 3 large | Carrots cut roughly |
| 2 each | Tomatoes, chopped |
| 1 bunch | Herb mélange, tied with butchers twine (rosemary, thyme, oregano – equal amounts) |
| 10 each | Bay leaf, small handful |
| 1 Cup | Chicken Stock, roasted |
| 1 bottle | Dark beer, (Porter) |
| 4 Tbs. | Balsamic vinegar |

## *Second part:*

| | |
|---|---|
| ½ Cup | Grape must (see notes) |
| 1 Cup | Tobacco flour, see notes |
| 1 each | Red onions, sliced very thin on a rotatory slicer |
| As needed | Frying Oil, use Safflower oil for best results |
| As needed | Sea salt (for the onions) |
| 1 Cup | Roquefort, crumbled |
| 2 dozen | Olives |
| 1 Cup | Honey Mustard sauce, prepared, store bought |

**Directions:**

Mix the pre-seasons together in a small bowl with a fork and use this to completely cover the pork ahead of time before cooking. Rub it in well and press into the flesh. In a pot or pan large enough for your roast, I use a Dutch oven, heat on medium heat atop the stove. Then place the meat in the pan to sear the spices to the meat. Cook the roast until dark brown. As this is cooking fill the crock pot.

Place the veggies on the bottom of the crock pot. Remove the roast from the Dutch oven after all the pork is seared very brown. Nestle it unto the top of the veggies and then add the beer and the stock around the edges (but not on top the roast). Place the herbs (tied in a bundle) atop the roast. Turn the crock pot on low or simmer overnight….about 10 hours. I usually start this very late at night so in the morning the entire house has the scent of roasted meats. This keeps me very excited about getting home that night and having dinner with family and friends.

Remove the roast; it will be much smaller than what it was when it went in. Drain for five minutes before cutting into chunks for the dinner plate (see the bottom picture). Save the veggies for plate garnishing. Place the juice into a very hot-wide pan, to reduce the original volume to almost dry over high heat. This will take a while depending on the pot you use. The wider the pot the faster the juices will dehydrate. Add the **Grape Must** to this sauce, reduce heat stir well and then cool once all incorporated. Place this sauce into a bottle with a fine tip (like a squeeze bottle for ketchup or mustard) and make decorative lines over the roast (and on the plate) as you see in the picture. Divide the roast evenly for 8 plates.- (see the picture below).

Toss the onions in the tobacco flour and shake the excess flour off the onions. Place into a deep fry pot with hot oil and cook for around four minutes, Drain, Season with a little more salt. Use for garnish on top the roast as seen in the picture below.

Set the mustard sauce on the top quadrant of the plate. Pile the cheese and the olives over top the sauce in a mound with celery leaves set on top for garnishes.

Place the divided roast on the plate and decorate the plate as seen in the picture below. Sauce the roast with the pan dripping sauce and decorate your plate as well.

### *Notes:*

***Grape Must*** is a super concentrated sauce made by reducing the juice from grapes into syrup. Use sparingly!

***Roquefort*** is actually sheep's milk cheese.

***Tobacco flour:*** Mix together 1 Cup of flour mixed with 2 Tbs. Smoked Paprika, 1 Tbs. Powdered Garlic, ½ Tsp. Sea salt, ½ Tsp. Cumin, 1/3 Tsp.. White Pepper.

*Finished Plate 10 Hour Pork*

# Turkey, Oatmeal and Quinoa meatloaf

Serves: 4

This recipe can also use the potato recipe that follows.

**Ingredient:**

| | |
|---|---|
| ¼ Cup | Quinoa salad (previous recipe), chop everything up |
| 20 oz. | Turkey, ground |
| 1 Tbs. | Tomato paste |
| 1 Tbs. | Hot pepper sauce |
| 2 Tbs. | Worcestershire sauce |
| 2 each | Eggs |
| 1 Cup | Oatmeal, instant |
| 1 ½ Tsp. | Seasalt |
| 1 Tsp. | Black pepper, ground |

\*\*\*

| | |
|---|---|
| 2 Tbs. | Brown sugar |
| 2 Tsp. | Worcestershire sauce |

Continued...

*This meatloaf is finished with roasted potato mélange seasoned with fresh herbs.*

**Directions:**

Preheat an oven to 375 degrees.

Chop the *Quinoa* salad up into what you would consider proper for a meatloaf. Leave out the dressing of course. Stir the ground turkey, cooked quinoa salad, tomato paste, hot sauce, 2 Tbs. Worcestershire, eggs, oatmeal, salt and pepper in a large bowl until well combined. The mixture will be wet and hard to shape. Shape into a loaf on a foil lined baking sheet. Combine the brown sugar, 2 Tsp. Worcestershire in a small bowl. Rub this paste over the top of the meatloaf.

Bake in the preheated oven until no longer pink in the center, about 50 minutes. Cook until the internal temperature reaches at least 150 degrees F. Let the meatloaf cool for 10 minutes before slicing and serving. See the second picture and set up as it appears.

***Optional:*** *rather than potatoes....*

Serve with vegan red curry or with an arugula, apple (or blueberry), lemon-EVO and goat cheese salad (recipes follow). Use one of the dressing recipes in this book to use for a little flavor boost.

# Gluten Free Meatloaf

*Serves 4 to 6*

**Ingredients:**

| | |
|---|---|
| 1 lb. | Pork, ground - shoulder cut |
| 1 lb. | Turkey meat, ground |
| 1 Tsp. | Salt & Pepper |
| 2 Tbs. | Thyme, fresh, chopped |
| 2 each | Eggs |
| 2 Tbs. | Mrs. Dash seasons |
| 1 Tsp. | Garlic powder |

| | |
|---|---|
| 1 Tsp. | Onion powder |
| 4 oz. | Roasted peppers, red, chopped fine |
| ¾ Cup | Oatmeal, instant, might need more |
| 4 oz. | EVO |
| 4 Cups | Spinach, baby |
| ½ Cup | Shallots, diced |
| 1 Cup | Pearl onions, whole and split if large |
| 2 Cups | Chicken stock, canned |
| 2 Cups | Caramelized onions, *see recipe that follows* |

**Directions:**

Preheat an oven to 375 degrees.

Mix the pork and turkey with the next 6 ingredients. Mix well to get the spices mixed in completely. Add the roasted peppers and the oatmeal. Let the oatmeal absorb the meat mix for 20 minutes. Shape into a loaf. Place half the EVO in a non-stick skillet. Heat the oil and brown the loaf in the oil to give it color.

Place the loaf on a baking sheet and roast in a 375 degree oven for 50 minutes. Cook and let rest on the counter to prepare the spinach.

To cook the spinach, heat the oil and add the spinach until it wilts. Remove and let the spinach drain. Warm the onions in the same pan and cook for 3 minutes on low. Serve with another starch (you could substitute the Olive oil braised greens found after this recipe).

Deglaze the sauce pan with the stock. Let cook several minutes to gather all the flavors in the stock. Reduce the deglazing juices to make into a sauce that you can use with this recipe.

Serve with the other recipes and make sure you tell everyone this isn't beef. Most people won't be able to tell.

GF Meatloaf

**Additional Recipe:**

# Vegan Caramelized Onions:

Serves: 4

*This recipe is paired with the others to follow…. .see the following recipes to complete an entire dish that you are going to love. Or, use this for many other recipes like the meatloaf recipe in this book.*

### Ingredients:

| | |
|---|---|
| 1 Tbs. | Avocado (vegan) butter |
| 1 each | Yellow onion, sliced |
| 1 Tbs. | Coconut sugar (or use Agave) |
| Pinch | Seasalt or low-sodium salt |
| 1 Tbs. | Balsamic vinegar |
| 2 each | Garlic, minced |
| 2 Tsp. | Thyme, fresh |
| 1 Tbs. | Crushed red pepper |

### Directions:

Cut the large yellow onion into thick slices.

Over medium-low heat, melt the plant-based butter in a thick-bottomed pan. Add onions and cook for 10 minutes. Add salt and the coconut sugar, then reduce the heat and continue to cook the onions for 30 minutes to one hour until they are deep amber (in color). Stir them often enough so that they don't burn.

Add the balsamic vinegar, thyme, and garlic. Cook for an additional 3 minutes and set aside.

Use for topping on meatloaf slices, Vegan burgers, chicken, fish fillets, on top polenta, salads (like warm potato salad), or as a filling for raviolis, etc.…

*See other recipes in this book that call for caramelized onions.*

# Chapter Three:
## *Veggies and such...*

*There are many ways to make meals healthier. Limit fats, sugars and salt and include plenty of vegetables, fruit, grains, lean meats and low-fat dairy in your cooking. Foods with **added** fats, sugars or salt are less healthy than food in which these are found naturally*

*For example, **non-stick cookware** can be used to reduce the need for cooking oil. Vegetables can also be microwaved or steamed instead of boiling to keep valuable nutrition.*

## Vegan Potatoes

Serves: 8

*Here is a new twist on one of our favorite foods. Potatoes and other **resistant starches** should be on your dinner table all the time. But when it comes to vitamins and minerals, orange sweet potatoes are vitamin A superstars.*

### Ingredients:

| | |
|---|---|
| 3 lb. | Yukon gold potatoes, sliced thin |
| 1 each | Onion, white or yellow, sliced thin |
| To taste | Pepper, cracked |
| 2 Tsp. | Onion powder |
| ½ Cup | Cashews, chopped |
| 1 Tbs. | Mustard |
| ½ each | Lemon juice, fresh squeezed |
| ½ Cup | Nutritional Yeast |
| 1.5 cups | Water |

**Directions:**

Preheat oven to 350 degrees. Mandolin slice potatoes and onion on the same thickness. Place the potatoes into a bowl of water, so they don't brown while you are doing the rest of the recipe.

Mix the onion powder, cashews, mustard, lemon juice, Nutritional Yeast, and water in a blender. Grind well. Layer two layers of potatoes and one layer of onions in a large casserole baking dish. Pour half of this "sauce" over the sliced potatoes and onions.

Layer another layer of potatoes and onion and then the remaining potatoes. Pour the rest of the sauce over the top. Cover with a piece of tin foil. Bake for 90 minutes. Take the foil off and bake for another 10 minutes to brown lightly.

# Home-style Veggie pot

*This is a recipe that can be cooked ahead of dinner time, cooled and reheated when you are ready to serve. Southern Greens are mustard greens or whatever you find like Black Cabbage or Kale.*

Serves: 6

**Ingredients:**

| | |
|---|---|
| 4 Cups | Veggie stock |
| 2 Cups | Southern greens, (or Tuscan Kale) cut inch pieces |
| 3 Tbs. | Oil |
| 1 each | Onion, white, chopped |
| 3 each | Garlic, crushed |
| 1 each | Tomato, diced |
| 1 Tbs. | Garlic powder |
| 2 Tbs. | Liquid smoke |
| 1 Tsp. | Paprika, smoked |
| 2 Tbs. | Vegan bacon bits |
| As needed | Salt and course ground Black Pepper |

**Directions:**

Start this recipe off by browning the onions then, add the garlic so it doesn't burn. Toss in the Southern greens and let them cook, weeping the leaves. "The more you cook them the better", Granny says. Turning the leaves constantly add the liquids and let cook for up to 3 hours on low heat.

Add the rest of the ingredients. Stirring constantly. End with the spices so you can add only enough to help flavors meld and compliment each other.
Serve along side rice dishes and Chickpeas. You can cool and use later after reheating.

# Brussel Sprouts with Guarapo – Citrus Dressing

Serves: 4

Good to use for cold chicken salad dressing. Try this with Tuna for salad dressing instead of mayo.

**Ingredients:**

| | |
|---|---|
| 1 Cup | Agave Syrup |
| 5 each | Mint leaves |
| .5 bunch | Cilantro leaves, chopped |
| 3 each | Chilies, baby sweet |
| 1 Tsp. | Red chili flakes |
| Pinch | Salt |
| 2 oz. | Triple sec |
| 1 oz. | Vodka citron flavored |
| 4 each | Lemon, lime and orange, Zest and juice |
| 3-4 Cups | Brussel sprout, leaves only |

| | |
|---|---|
| As needed | Oil for wok stir-frying |
| .25 Cup | Fakeon, "fake bacon" |
| As needed | Salt |

**Directions:**

Mix all ingredients together. Simmer on low for 15 minutes. Cool and use for the Brussels when they come out of the oil.

Heat the oil in a wok. Add the leaves and quickly sauté them to just soft. About 3 minutes.

Season add the "Fakeon". Remove from wok to a bowl. Drizzle the syrup over them toss in bowl and place on serving plates. Garnish with more fresh herbs.

# Cauliflower Mango and Chili, Lime Marinade

This makes for a perfect snack when you just need something sassy and good tasting.

Serves: 4

**Ingredients:**

| | |
|---|---|
| 1 oz. | Lime juice |
| 1 oz. | Chili paste |
| 2 Tbs. | Garlic, crushed |
| 1 Tbs. | Brown sugar |
| 1 Tsp. | Fish sauce |
| 2 Tbs. | Cilantro, copped |
| 1 Tsp. | Salt |
| 2 oz. | Evo |
| 1 each | Cauliflower, large head, about 2 inches thick. |
| 1 Cup | Mango, chunks |
| As needed | Water |
| As needed | Salt |
| As needed | EVO |

**Directions:**

Cut the Cauliflower straight through the head (about 2 inches thick)....into "steaks". Have a pot of salted water (large enough for the cauliflower) boiling. Add a lot of salt. Cook the steaks tender..... when you can easily insert a fork into the thickest part of the steak .... they are done.

Cool slightly. Place in a container so you can soak/marinate the steaks for a while. Drain and place is a super-hot skillet and sear the steaks. They will cook to the proper softness in 3 minutes. Place on a serving plate topped with mango chunks and baby lettuces as a garnish around the plate. Add some extra sauce for the plate if needed..

**Notes:**

Drizzle with a creamy Pineapple Ranch dressing.


# Pineapple Ranch Dressing

Serves: 6

*Dressing:*

**Ingredients:**

| | |
|---|---|
| 6 each | Pineapple rings, grilled |
| 1 Cup | Ranch dressing, jarred, packaged |
| 2 oz. | Coconut cream |
| 1 oz. | Orange juice concentrate |
| 1 oz. | Lemon juice |

**Directions:**

Mix all dressing ingredients together and blend until all are smooth. Use for the upper recipe. Use as a dip or drizzle over top right before serving.

# Roasted Beet-Mango Relish

*Roasted beet relish interspersed with mango and the earthy cumin flavors highlighted with the lime zest and juice helps bring out the best of these antioxidant-rich recipe ingredients. This recipe is good warm or cold as a salad. I use this as a base to make fashionable stacked-food plates that make it look like 4-star cuisine.*

### Beets and Mangoes are found to be...

- Mangos are **Rich** in vitamin C, vitamin A precursors, and **antioxidants**. A 1-cup serving of mango contains about 100 calories and some vitamin C, calcium, vitamin E and vitamin A.

- Support healthy blood pressure

- Promote nitric oxide production, which supports cardiovascular health

- Protect against DNA damage. **Folate** - *Mangoes also contain folate, or* **vitamin B** *-- This vitamin plays an important role in helping your body produce proteins and DNA -- the building blocks of newborn cells.*

- *For this reason, getting enough folate is especially important for expectant mothers, because they need to meet the needs of the developing baby's rapidly-dividing cells. A cup of mango provides 71 micrograms of folate, or 18 percent of the folate you need each day.*

- Beets support a healthy inflammatory response. The key antioxidant ingredients that may help support your body's inflammatory response... Beets with other fruits like Kiwi, Blueberries, or a few slices of mango can add an extra touch of sweetness to help curb your sugar cravings.

**Ingredients:**

| | |
|---|---|
| 3 Cups | Beets, cubed, peeled (**2 large or 3 small beets) |
| 2 Tsp. | Avocado oil |
| ¼ Tsp. | Sea salt |
| ½ Tsp. | Cumin, ground, plus more for garnishing |
| 1-2 Tsp. | Agave syrup |
| 1 each | Mango, diced (added later) |
| ½ Tsp. | Lime zest |
| 1-2 Tbs. | Lime juice |
| As you like | Fresh cilantro |

**Directions:**

Heat oven to 375 degrees F (190 C) and line a baking sheet with parchment paper. Add peeled, cubed beets to a medium mixing bowl along with avocado oil, salt, and cumin.

Roast beets for 35-40 minutes, or until fork tender and slightly golden brown. Toss, or fold over the beets unto themselves, once at the 20-minute mark to ensure even baking. The longer they bake the more tender and caramelized they become. They are a little sweeter and do change color quicker after heating more than this suggested timetable, be careful not to overcook, or they can become crispy from the internal sugar content.

Once roasted, add back to the mixing bowl from earlier and season with maple syrup, lime zest, and lime juice, and mix. Taste and adjust flavor as needed, adding more lime juice for acidity, lime zest for citrus flavor, cumin for smokiness, salt to taste, or maple syrup for sweetness.

Add the ripe mangoes. Garnish with fresh cilantro, if desired.

# Dukkah Cauliflower

Serves: 4 to 6 as an appetizer or side dish

**Ingredients:**

| | |
|---|---|
| 2 Tbs. | Garlic, minced |
| 3 Tbs. | Olive oil |
| 1 large | Cauliflower, head, separated into florets |
| ⅓ Cup | Parmesan cheese, grated |
| To taste | Seasalt and ground black pepper |
| 1 Tbs. | Parsley, chopped |

## Second part of recipe: *Dukkah*

| ⅓ Cup  | Hazelnuts, toasted |
|---|---|
| ¼ Cup  | Sesame seeds, toasted |
| 1 Tbs. | Coriander seeds, toasted |
| 1 Tbs. | Cumin seeds, toasted |
| ½ Tbs. | Black pepper, ground |
| ½ Tsp. | Sea salt, flaked |

## Directions:

Preheat the oven to 450 degrees F. Spray a large casserole dish with pan spray. Place the olive oil and garlic in a large resealable bag. Add cauliflower, and shake to mix. Pour into the prepared casserole dish, and season with salt and pepper to taste.

Bake for 25 minutes, stirring halfway through. Top with Parmesan cheese and parsley, and broil for 3 to 5 minutes, until golden brown.

When you remove from the oven, place on plate and toss the Dukkah spice blend over the top as a flavorful garnish.

## *Second part:* Dukkah - spice blend

Preheat the oven to 350 degrees F. Place the hazelnuts on a baking sheet, and bake for about 5 minutes. While the nuts are still hot, pour them onto a towel. Fold the towel over them to cover, and rub vigorously to remove the skins. Set aside after you remove their skins and cool.

In a dry skillet over medium heat, toast the sesame seeds until light golden brown. Pour into a medium bowl, so they will not continue toasting. In the same skillet, toast the coriander and cumin seeds while shaking the pan or stirring occasionally until they begin to pop. Transfer to a coffee grinder and process until smooth. Then pour into the bowl with the sesame seeds. Place the cooled hazelnuts into a food processor, and process until finely ground. Stir into the bowl with the spices. Season with salt and pepper, and mix well.

Use this to top off many recipes. The added **protein** and flavor can be used in any dish of bland veggies.

# Olive Oil Braised Greens

*Use this recipe paired with any pork, chicken or seafood recipes.*

*Serves: 4*

**Ingredients:**

| | |
|---|---|
| 2 lbs. | Swiss chard or baby Bok Choy |
| To taste | Olive oil |
| 2 Tsp. | Garlic, crushed |
| 1 Tbs. | Lemon juice |
| To taste | Salt |
| ½ Cup | Mint leaves |
| 1 Tbs. | Dill |

**Directions:**

Sauté the greens until soft in the olive oil. Drain well.

Then warm some oil and heat the garlic. Pour the garlic, lemon juice and seasons over the greens.

Toss openly to get all the spices incorporated well.

Add the mint and dill.

Serve as cold salad or a base to elevate another food entrée off the plate for a more stylish presentation.

*Pork Schnitzel atop Braised greens*

# Plantain Curry Stew

Serves: 2-4

**Ingredients:**

| | |
|---|---|
| 6 each | Plantain, green |
| 1 each | Sweet potato, cleaned, diced (1 cup |
| 12 oz. | Kidney beans, canned, cooked |
| 2 each | Onion, chopped well |
| 1/3 Cup | Scallion, chopped |
| ¼ Cup each | Bell peppers, three colors, diced |
| 2 16 oz. can | Coconut milk, skim top fat for sautéing veggies |
| 1 bunch | Callaloo, or Kale |
| 2 each | Tomato, diced |
| 1 Tbs. | Curry powder |
| 1 Tsp. | Ginger |
| 2 Tbs. | Garlic |
| 1 Tsp. | Black pepper |
| 2 Tbs. | Thyme, fresh, chopped |
| 1 Tsp. | Coriander, ground |
| 1 Tsp. | Salt |
| 1 Cup | Water |
| 3 Tbs. | Coconut cream, (from the cans of milk) |
| 1 each | Scotch bonnet, chopped extremely fine |

**Directions:**

Skim the coconut fat from the coconut milk in the can. Heat the fat and use to sauté the veggies. Cook until well softened. Add the beans and then the Callaloo, stew until well softened. Add the liquids then let cook another 20 minutes. Season. Add the chili.

Let cook a total of an hour. Serve in a bowl filled with veggies from the pot.

**Notes:**

Plantains are a good source of **Resistant Starch**[20].

---

20    https://www.healthline.com/nutrition/resistant-starch-101

# Charred Beans
Serves: 4

**Ingredients:**

| | |
|---|---|
| 1 bunch | Chinese Long beans, cut after steaming in water |
| As needed | Salted water |
| ½ Cup | Red bell pepper, jully |
| ½ Cup | Pineapple, no husk and sliced thin |
| 1 Cup | Red onion petals, charred, (see notes before tossing other ingredients) |
| ¼ Cup | Cilantro, rough chopped |
| 10 each | Plum Tomatoes, ¼'ed, (Salted first) |
| 1 Tsp. | Salt |
| 1-2 Tsp. | Cumin, (depending on your tastes) |
| 1-2 Tbs. | Sage, chopped well (depending on your tastes) |

**Directions:**

*First,* get a pot of water large enough to cook the long beans. Get another container that will hold the beans and fill it with ice water. Heat the pot of water to a boil, add the beans and let cook 3 to 5 minutes until they turn bright green. Remove and toss into the other pot of iced water. This will shock the beans, stopping the cooking process and set the color of the beans so they don't turn a drab color of grayish green.

Next, get the beans cut into manageable pieces to eat, something like 2-3 inches long. Toss with the other ingredients in the top part of the recipe. Save till after you make the sauce.

Sauce: In the same wok that you used to cook the petals, see notes below, heat the wok to high heat. Using a gas stove is best for this. Turn on the exhaust fan above the stove as well. Toss in the salted tomatoes and don't move them until they are noticeably darkened. Season with the other ingredients toss to let the tomatoes simmer in their own juice. Remove and keep this warm.

Next: Clean out the wok, heat again on medium high heat. Toss the shocked beans in. Add the rest of the ingredients and toss to warm. Maybe 3 minutes, remove to a serving plate. Top with the stewed tomatoes.

**Notes:**

To make the onion petals; take a baseball size onion; trim off the skin and quarter it down the center. Pull apart the individual "petals" as you separate the onion into slices. Heat a wok to gray hot, rub with a slight amount of oil and toss in the petals. Let cook and they will smoke a little. Get some char on the petals, remove and add to the rest of the dish.

# Vegan Red Lentil Curry

This is such a great example of **anti-Cancer ingredients** packed into one recipe. *Vegan* and *Gluten-Free*. And Lentils are *Starch Resistant*[21].

Serves: 4-6

**Ingredients:**

| | |
|---|---|
| 2 Tbs. | Coconut oil |
| 4 cloves | Garlic, minced |
| 2 inch | Ginger, piece of fresh, peeled and minced fine |
| 1 Tbs. | Turmeric, fresh (you should be able to find in Asian markets) |
| 1 each | Serrano peppers, finely chopped |
| 1 Tsp. | Cumin, toasted and ground |
| ½ Tsp. | Coriander, ground |
| 1 Tsp. | Curry powder |
| 1 Tsp. | Garam masala |
| 1 Cup | Red lentils, (I use Beluga (*black*) lentils ) |
| 2 Cups | Vegetable broth |
| 14 oz. | Tomatoes, crushed in the can |
| 14-oz. | Coconut milk |
| 3 Tbs. | Avocado butter |

---

21  https://www.healthline.com/nutrition/resistant-starch-101

| | |
|---|---|
| ½ each | Lime, juiced |
| To taste | Sea salt |
| To taste | Black pepper (add later) |
| ½ Cup | Cilantro, fresh, roughly chopped |

**Directions:**

Rinse the lentils until the water runs clear. Let drain well.

Heat a large, deep skillet or large saucepan over medium-high heat and add the coconut oil. You might need more oil depending on the size of the pan. Use at least an 8 inch, heavy-bottom pot. Once the oil is heated and is shimmering, lower heat to medium and add the garlic, ginger, turmeric, and Serrano pepper and cook for 2 minutes, stirring frequently to prevent garlic from burning.

After they are softened by sautéing, add the cumin, coriander, chili powder, curry powder, Garam masala, and cook for 1 minute until fragrant. You will notice the earthy smell rising from the pan when they are cooked long enough.

Stir in the lentils, vegetable broth, and the crushed tomatoes and mix well. Reduce the heat to low and cover the pan with a lid. Simmer for 20-25 minutes until the lentils are cooked through and have softened. If you find that the lentils are not quite soft after 25 minutes, add a few spoons more of broth or water and cook for another 5 minutes.

Remove the lid and stir in the coconut milk and avocado butter. Continue cooking on low heat, uncovered for 5-7 minutes. Finally, stir in the lime juice and cilantro, and turn off the heat. Taste and season if needed with the salt and pepper.

### *Notes:*

I usually make my lentils creamier by using an immersion blender to lightly purée the curry. This makes for a nice hearty stew (served with Basmati rice) or puree more to a pulse to make a dip for chips and flat breads.

# Vegan Red Curry sauce

**Ingredients:**

| | |
|---|---|
| 4 Tbs. | Red curry |
| 1/2 Cup | Coconut milk |
| 1 Cup | Pineapple juice |
| 1 Tsp. | Fish sauce |
| 1/4 lb. | Oven-roasted tomatoes |
| 1 oz. | Mirin (sweetened sake) |
| 1 Tbs. | Sherry wine |
| 1 Tbs. | Triple sec |
| 2 oz. | Mango puree |
| To thicken | Cornstarch (start with 3 Tbs.) |
| Water | As needed |

**Directions:**

Place all ingredients in a pot except for the cornstarch. Boil and then reduce heat to a simmer for five minutes.

Then mix the cornstarch and water together. Pour into the sauce a little at a time as the sauce simmers to a thickened consistency you will enjoy.

Use for various seafood, meats and chicken dishes.

# *Resistant starch[22]:*

What is it? And why is it so *good for you*?

*Lentils* are a good source of resistant starches. Where is RS found on your menus?

- RS is found in starchy plant foods such as:
  - Beans/legumes
  - Starchy fruits and vegetables (like bananas).
  - Whole grains - unprocessed kernels and seeds.
  - Cooked then cooled foods (such as potatoes and rice)

**Potatoes** also have a type of resistant starch known as retrograde starch. When you cook and then cool potatoes, the starch molecules shuffle themselves around into a different structure.

Resistant starch is a type of starch that isn't fully broken down and absorbed, but rather turns into short-chain fatty acids by bacteria in your intestine.

Choose whole, unprocessed sources of carbohydrate such as whole grains, fruits, vegetables, and beans/legumes, to get the most from resistant starch.

Some starch — known as resistant starch (RS) — isn't fully absorbed in the small intestine. Instead, RS makes its way to the large intestine (colon), where intestinal bacteria ferment it.

When RS is fermented in the large intestine, your body processes short chain fatty acids for energy.

Less-processed foods offer less energy than refined foods. In other words, although whole and processed foods may contain the same amount of calories, we absorb fewer calories of energy from whole foods.

---
22    https://www.healthline.com/nutrition/resistant-starch-101

RS is incompletely digested, we only extract about 2 calories of energy per gram (versus about 4 calories per gram from other refined starches). That means you can eat more and your body processes the food resulting in half the calories absorbed.

So to get the most benefits from RS, we need to consume it in whole food cooked without processing like grinding wheat kernels into flour.

***Other good tendencies of RS foods:***

RS foods improved blood fats.

RS (in laboratory studies) has helped to *lower* blood *cholesterol* and fats, while also decreasing the production of new fat cells. RS consumption improves insulin sensitivity lowering blood fats, which also improves insulin sensitivity. Also, since SCFAs[23] (*Short Chain fatty Acids*) can inhibit the breakdown of carbohydrates, RS can increase the amount of fat we utilize to produce energy that our bodies can use.

RS don't get digested into blood sugar, meaning it doesn't raise insulin levels in our bodies in response. RS will also improve insulin sensitivity via alterations in fatty acid flux between muscle and fat cells.

### *Plantains:*

Green plantains are **a good source of resistant starch**, a type of dietary fiber that helps you feel full, doesn't raise blood sugar, and feeds the good bacteria that keep your gut healthy.
Products from Unripe Plantain Flour Help **Lowering Cholesterol and Controlling Blood Sugar**. Unripe plantain is a natural source of resistant starch that helps to reduce blood glucose levels, so it is considered an excellent ingredient for food fortification.

23   https://www.healthline.com/nutrition/short-chain-fatty-acids-101

# How to make a Gluten Free - Vegan Pasta

**Ingredients:**

| | |
|---|---|
| 2 Tbs. | Flaxseed meal (toasted seeds ground fine) |
| 6 Tbs. | Warm water (90 degrees F) |
| 1.5 Cups | Chickpea flour |
| ¼ Cup | Tapioca flour |
| ½ Tsp. | Sea salt |
| 2 Tsp. | EVO olive oil |

**Directions:**

Mix the flaxseed and warm water in a small bowl and set aside for about 10 minutes, or until thickened.

Meanwhile, whisk together the chickpea flour, tapioca flour, and salt in a large bowl. Make a well in the middle of the dry ingredients and add the flaxseed and water mixture. Stir until large crumbles form, and then add the oil and knead with your hands until the dough comes together and can be formed into a ball.

Wrap the dough in plastic wrap and set aside for 20-30 minutes.

Bring a pot of salted water to a boil. Dust a large surface, your hands, and a rolling pin with chickpea flour, and roll the dough out until very thin. The dough is tough, so this will be a bit of a workout.

Place in a pasta rolling machine and cut the pasta style you like. Fettuccine cut is the best for this recipe.

Once the water has come to a rolling boil in a large pot, add the pasta and cook for 1-3 minutes. If the pasta is cooked for too long, it will begin to break into pieces. Drain and toss to serve hot with your sauce. I topped this with pan-seared scallops.

Pan-Seared Scallops over GF pasta

After the 1860's Pineapples were grown in the Keys on the Island just a few miles from where I live now. This recipe is a tribute to those families that braved the weather and conditions of living in the Keys without air conditioning.

I have always admired the people that found ways to survive hurricanes and our year-long heat waves. It is amazing when you think about it. I could not walk down the street a mile without passing out. These are some sturdy people that ate healthy, filling food.

# 100 Year Fennel Salad

Serves: 6-10

**Ingredients:**

***Pickling brine:***

| | |
|---|---|
| 1 Pt. | Malt vinegar |
| 1 Cup | Sugar |
| 1/2 Cup | Salt |
| As needed | Water |
| 3 each | Bay leaf |
| 2 doz. | Black peppercorns |
| 1 Cup | Celery leaves |
| 1 each | Cinnamon stick |
| 12 each | Fennel bulbs, grilled, cooled, split |
| 2 each | Oranges, split and grilled |
| 2 each | Red Onion, sliced into 1/3'eds, grilled |
| 1/2 each | Pineapple, ripe, cut into 1/2 inch wedges, grilled |

\*\*\*

***Salad:***

| | |
|---|---|
| 1 each | Fennel, from above recipe, split |
| 1 Cup | Baby greens |
| 1/2 Cup | Kale, baby |
| 1/2 Cup | Arugula |
| 1/2 Cup | Frisee, baby endives |
| 2 each | Baby sweet chilies, cut into rings |
| 1/2 Cup | Celery, cut on the bias |
| 1/3 Cup | Goat's cheese, crumbled |
| 3 oz. | Lemon juice, fresh |
| 5 oz. | EVO |
| 1 Tsp. | Seasalt |
| 1/2 Tsp. | Red chili flakes |

**Directions:**

First make the brine. Cook the vinegar, sugar and salt over the stove until all is dissolved. Add the rest of the ingredients and let cook to the fennel is soft enough to pierce with a fork. Add enough water to cover the ingredients.

*\*\*\* This can be placed in your refrigerator for months. At the turn of the last century we didn't have refrigeration and this recipe was good to hold at room temperature for days. That is what makes this a great dish for the Florida Keys and places where pickling foods are required so there was something to eat throughout the year.*

*Luckily we have refrigeration now and this is more a tribute recipe than a necessary survival recipe.*

Cool, remove, drain the pickled ingredients. Arrange on serving plates decorated with the dispersed salad ingredients. Mix the Lemon juice EVO and Seasons. Shake well. Garnish with the rest of the ingredients. Sprinkle the cheese around the plate and apply the dressing.

Composed pickled Fennel salad

# Chapter Four:
## Sweet Stuff

# Vegan Chocolate pudding

Serves: 2-4 people

**Ingredients:**

¼ Cup         Cacao powder or unsweetened cocoa powder
3 Tbs.        Coconut syrup
2 Tbs.        Coke syrup, (from the dispenser tank/box)
1/2 Tsp.      Cinnamon, ground
1 pinch       Sea salt
1.5 Cups      Vanilla flavored Almond milk (use coconut milk for a creamier texture)
½ Cup         Chia seeds

**Directions:**

To a small mixing bowl add cacao powder (sift first to reduce clumps), syrups, ground cinnamon, salt, and whisk to combine. Then add a little dairy-free milk at a time and whisk until a paste forms. Then add remaining dairy-free milk and whisk until smooth.

Add chia seeds and whisk once more to combine. Then cover and refrigerate overnight, or at least 3-5 hours (until it's achieved a pudding-like consistency).

Leftovers keep covered in the fridge for 4-5 days, though best when fresh. Serve chilled with desired toppings ... coconut (milk)-whipped cream.

# Vegan Pudding

Serves: 4

## Ingredients:

| | |
|---|---|
| 12 oz. | Tofu, *Silken* |
| ½ Cup | Cocoa powder, unsweetened organic |
| 2 oz. | Maple syrup, real not commercial |
| 2 Tbs. | Coconut syrup, organic |
| 1 Tsp. | Vanilla extract, organic |
| 1 Tbs. | Jameson Irish Whiskey |
| 2 Tbs. | Coconut flakes, toasted lightly |

## Directions:

Place silken tofu in a fine mesh strainer and allow to drain for 20 minutes to remove excess water. Place tofu & remaining ingredients in a food processor and process until smooth and creamy.

Check for sweetness.

Chill pudding in the refrigerator for 1 hour before serving.

Top with toasted coconut flakes.

Or, top with shaved chocolate shavings.

# Banana "bread" smoothie

Serves: 2

**Ingredients:**

| | |
|---|---|
| 2 Cups | Almond milk, vanilla flavored |
| ¼ Cup | Almonds, toasted if you want a little different flavor |
| 2 each | Banana, frozen |
| 1 Tsp. | Vanilla extract |
| 1 Tsp. | Cinnamon |
| ¼ Tsp. | Allspice |
| 4 each | Medjool Dates, these give the shake a cakey texture. |
| Dash | Salt |
| ½ Cup | Ice cubes |

**Directions:**

Put everything in a blender and process smoothly. Place in a cool glass.

Garnish the rim of the glass and top of the full glass with cinnamon and sugar mixture for a little "pop" in flavor.

# Breakfast Quinoa with Blueberries

*With cinnamon, brown sugar, vanilla, and sweet blueberries, this creamy breakfast porridge is tasty, satisfying, and good for you!*

Serves: 4

**Ingredients:**

| | |
|---|---|
| 1 Cup | Water |
| 1.5 Cups | Milk (almond, or coconut), plus more for serving |
| 1 Tsp. | Vanilla extract |
| 1 Cup | Quinoa, rinsed well |
| 1 Tsp. | Salt |
| 3 Tbs. | Brown sugar, (plus more for serving- as you like) |
| ¼ Tsp. | Cinnamon, ground. |

| ½ Tsp. | Cardamom, ground. |
| ¾ Cup | Blueberries, crush half of them |
| As needed | Almonds, sliced or chopped toasted pecans, for topping |

**Directions:**

In a heavy-bottomed saucepan, combine water, 1-1/2 cups milk, vanilla extract, rinsed quinoa, and salt. Bring to a boil over medium-high heat. Reduce heat...

Cook about 22 minutes on low heat. Cook almost dry.

Stir in 3 tablespoons brown sugar and the ground cinnamon and cardamom. Re-cover and continue to simmer for about 3 minutes, until all the liquid has been absorbed.

Remove from heat and gently fold in whole and crushed blueberries.

Serve, topped with extra brown sugar and almonds nuts.

# Chapter Five:

## *FYI:*

This is that section of the book that serious **Culinary Eggheads** will love.

### [The best protein food substitute ~ Beans!]()

*Dried beans, peas and lentils — a.k.a. legumes or pulses (a puree) — are a vital food source and one of the world's oldest cultivated crops. Evidence of cultivation goes back more than 7,000 years in some parts of the world.*

*An excellent source of protein, dietary fiber and complex carbohydrates, legumes and pulses are flavorful, nutritionally dense, inexpensive and versatile. What more could you ask for?*

Ever had a craving for Eyes of Goat, Tongues of Fire, or Mortgage Lifters? These are just a few of the outrageously named, yet delicious heirloom bean varieties that are grown regionally throughout the U.S. in addition to widely available favorites like black, pinto and kidney beans. Dried beans, peas and lentils are simply mature beans that are dried and then removed from their pods; look for all kinds in the bulk section and grocery aisles. We think there's a chance they could be the perfect food.

## Bean Cookin' 101

Cooking dried beans takes more time than opening a can, but you'll be richly rewarded with superior flavor and texture. They're a superb value too! Here's how.

Sort: Arrange dried beans on a sheet pan or clean kitchen towel and sort through them to pick out any shriveled or broken beans, stones or debris.

Rinse: In cold, running water.

Soak: Soaking beans before cooking helps to remove some of those indigestible sugars that cause flatulence. There are two simple ways to get the job done:

Regular soak: Put beans into a large bowl and cover with 2 to 3 inches of cool water. Set aside at room temperature for 8 hours or overnight; drain well.

Quick soak: Put beans into a large pot and cover with 2 to 3 inches of cool, water. Bring to a boil then boil briskly for 2 to 3 minutes. Cover and set aside off of the heat for 1 hour; drain well.

Cook: Put beans into a large pot and cover with 2 inches of water or stock. Slowly bring to a boil, *skimming off any foam on the surface*. Reduce heat, cover and simmer, stirring occasionally and adding more liquid if necessary, until beans are tender when mashed or pierced with a fork. Cooking times vary with the variety, age and size of beans; generally you're looking at about 1 to 2 hours.

## Pea and Lentil Cookin'

Sort and rinse dried peas and lentils as you would dry beans (see above). Then simply bring 1½ cups water or stock to a boil for each cup of dried lentils or peas. Once the liquid is boiling add the lentils or peas, return to a boil, and then reduce the heat and simmer, partially covered, until tender, 30 to 45 minutes.

Cooking Tip: Uncooked dried peas and lentils can be added directly to soups and stews, too. Just be sure there's enough liquid in the pot (about 1½ cups of liquid for every 1 cup of lentils or peas).

## Dictionary of Beans, Peas and Lentils

Here's a dictionary of our favorite varieties and how to make them do all the work:

Adzuki Beans

These little dark red beans are sweet and easy to digest. Splash them with tamari and barley malt or mix them with brown rice, scallions, mushrooms and celery for dynamite, protein-rich rice patties.

Anasazi Beans

This burgundy and white heirloom variety is popular in Southwestern recipes — especially soups.

Black Turtle Beans

Combine these little lovelies with cumin, garlic and orange juice or toss them with olive oil, cilantro and chopped veggies for two incomparable salads. Perfect for Cuban bean soups.

Black-Eyed Peas

Soft, quick-cooking bean. These creamy white, oval-shaped beans are ubiquitous in southeastern US states where they're a traditional New Year's dish.

Cannellini Beans

These smooth-textured beans are packed with nutty flavor. Add them to tomato-based soups like minestrone.

Garbanzo Beans (a.k.a. Chickpeas)

This prominent ingredient in Mediterranean, Middle Eastern, and East Indian dishes — has a mild but hearty flavor. Garbanzos are a good foil for strong spices like curry powder, cumin and cayenne pepper, so add them to salads, soups and pasta dishes.

Flageolet Beans

This creamy heirloom bean is used in French country cuisine as a side dish for lamb and poultry. Their delicate flavor is enhanced by aromatic onions, celery, carrots, garlic, bay leaves and thyme.

### Great Northern Beans

They're the largest commonly available white bean, but they're all soft and mild on the inside. Great Northern make for delicious baked beans or add them to soups and stews with longer cooking times.

### Green Lentils (a.k.a. French Lentils)

These lentils hold their shape well and have deep, rich flavor. They're an excellent addition to salads, spicy Indian Dal or simple lentils and rice.

### Green Split Peas

Give peas a chance! Split peas shine in soups where they're cooked until creamy to bring out their full, sweet flavor.

### Kidney Beans

These large, red beans are popular in chili, salads, soups and baked beans. Make sure to cook them until completely tender and cooked through to eliminate the gastric distress-causing toxin Phytohaemagglutinin (Kidney Bean Lectin) that's present in raw and undercooked kidney beans.

### Lima Beans

Add them to minestrone and other soups or combine them with corn and green beans for succotash.

### Lupini Beans

At Italian fairs and Spanish beer halls these beans are a popular snack. Technically a member of the pea family, these flat, coin-shaped, dull yellow seeds are second only to soybeans in plant protein content. Allow for a long soaking period and extended cooking time to reduce their potential for bitterness.

Mung Beans

You probably know mung beans for their sprouts, but the beans themselves are revered as a healing food. Mung beans range in color from greenish-brown to yellow to black and have delicate, sweet flavor. They need no pre-soaking, cook quickly and are easy to digest; you can't go wrong.

Pinto Beans

A favorite in Southwest and Mexican dishes -- these earthy beans have a delicious, creamy texture ideal for refrying. Combine with onions, chili powder, garlic and tomatoes as a filling for enchiladas or sauté cooked beans with olive oil, garlic and tamari.

Red Beans

These small, dark red beans are subtly sweet and hold their shape when cooked. They make a great choice for soups and chili and as a companion to rice.

Red Lentils

Don't be fooled by the name; this variety of lentil isn't really red. In fact, their soft pink color turns golden when cooked. Note that red lentils cook quickly and don't hold their shape so they're best in soups or purées or cooked until creamy with Italian seasonings.

Split Peas

While green peas are picked while immature and eaten fresh, dried peas are harvested when mature, stripped of their husks, split and dried. Split peas don't require pre-soaking and their mild flavor and creamy texture make good companions to garlic, onions, dill, curry and ginger.

# Lowering Your Cholesterol:

*Ask your doctor about limitation/elimination of these things I am going to list and what type of vitamin or supplement you should buy to help your body stay healthy during these lifestyle changes. These things are easy to find in a health food market.*

- Confirm with your doctor about what my suggestions will do to your health in combination with the drugs that he is prescribing for you.

    - *If your doctor does not suggest a diet change and only says you have to take pills to fix this, then he is a pill doctor and doesn't understand that your body can eventually fix this over time by changing what you eat….and, a little exercise.*

    - Anytime you see a recipe on-line or in a magazine that says "healthy" or **Mediterranean**-style it is probably good for you to use.

    - **Look for the RED HEART** healthy symbol, on packages … generally, it is true.

    - Learn to read labels on the sides of boxes. Look at: the portion size, saturated fat percentages, compare to other foods of the same nature and choose the one with lower saturated fat percentage!

        - *There are two main forms of cholesterol: "good cholesterol," also known as <u>HDL cholesterol</u>, and "<u>bad cholesterol</u>," also known as <u>LDL cholesterol</u>.*

        - Get **BEEF** out of your diet. If anything have a cheat once in a while.

            - Eat **fish**, SALMON or any other that is high in <u>**OMEGA 3**</u> oils actually will help you.

- The highest levels of **omega-3 fatty acids** are in cheap costing fish like: Mackerel, Lake trout, Herring, Sardines, Albacore tuna and Salmon
- ***Don't*** eat shrimp, lobster or crabs.
- ***Don't*** eat eggs, only eat whites for breakfast foods and baking.
- **Remove** COW's milk from what you are eating.
- Women should get protein rich substitutes, like adding whey protein to foods you like.
- Walnuts, almonds and other **tree nuts** can improve blood cholesterol. Rich in mono and polyunsaturated fatty acids, walnuts also help keep blood vessels healthy.

*Ask your doctor for a calcium boosting vitamin because you are going to need to eliminate drinking milk.*

- **Remove** Butter, use uns*aturated* spreads.
  - Any thing that is solid (like a spread) might be hydrogenated, meaning **SATURATED**. Only use **UNSATURATED** spreads.
  - Do not use any fat, oil or spread that is SOLID at room temperature (unless it is thickened with gelatin).
- Only use MONO-Saturated oil --- OLIVE oil is best and lowers your body's cholesterol.
- **Oatmeal** contains soluble fiber, which reduces your *low-density* lipoprotein (LDL), the "bad" cholesterol. Soluble fiber is also found in such foods as: *kidney beans, apples, pears, barley and prunes.*

- Avocados are a potent source of nutrients as well as *mono-unsaturated* fatty acid.

  - Also try **guacamole** with raw cut vegetables, such as cucumber slices. Using Caribbean or Florida *Avocados* are even better, they have **50 percent less** fat totally. The body's need for fats that you are limiting and avocados go a long way to fix the cravings.

# Fish:

*Remember that seafood is not only delicious; it can also provide wonderful benefits to your health.*

Fish is a very important part of a healthy diet. Fish and other seafood are the major sources of healthful long-chain omega-3 fats and are also rich in other nutrients such as vitamin D and selenium, high in protein, and low in saturated fat. There is strong evidence that eating fish or taking fish oil is good for the heart and blood vessels.

- An analysis of 20 studies involving hundreds of thousands of participants indicates that eating approximately <u>**one to two 3-ounce servings of fatty fish a week**</u>—salmon, herring, mackerel, anchovies, or sardines—*reduces* the risk of dying from heart disease by 36 percent.

Eating fish fights heart disease in several ways. The omega-3 fats in fish protect the heart against the development of erratic and potentially deadly cardiac rhythm disturbances. They also lower blood pressure and heart rate, improves blood vessel function and at higher doses, lowers triglycerides and may ease inflammation. The strong and consistent evidence for benefits is such that the Dietary Guidelines for Americans, the American Heart Association, and others suggest that everyone eat fish twice a week.

*Unfortunately, less than one in five Americans heeds that advice. About one-third of Americans eat seafood once a week, while nearly half eat fish only occasionally or not at all. Although some people may simply not like fish, the generally low consumption is likely also caused by other factors, including perceptions about cost, access to stores that sell fish, and uncertainty about how to prepare or cook fish.*

- Known or likely benefits: Eating about 2 grams per week of omega-3 fatty acids in fish, equal to about one or two servings of fatty fish a week, **reduces** the chances of **dying** from heart disease by more than **one-third**.

  - ***Possible benefits:*** Eating fish once or twice a week may also ***reduce*** the risk of stroke, depression, Alzheimer's disease, and other chronic conditions.

## Striking a Balance

First, reviewing data from the Environmental Protection Agency and elsewhere. They calculated that if 100,000 people ate farmed salmon twice a week for 70 years, 7,000 deaths might be prevented from heart disease.

Except perhaps for a few fish species, the scale tips in favor of fish consumption for women who are pregnant. High intake of mercury appears to hamper a baby's brain development. But low intake of omega-3 fats from fish is at least as dangerous. In a study of almost 12,000 pregnant women, children born to those who ate less than two servings of fish a week didn't do as well on tests of intelligence, behavior, and development as children born to mothers who ate fish at least twice a week.

> A study conducted by *Harvard* researchers showed that visual recognition scores in six-month-olds were highest in those whose mothers ate at least two servings of fish a week during pregnancy but who also had low mercury levels.

*Here's what the Environmental Protection Agency and Food and Drug Administration recommend for women who are or may become pregnant, nursing mothers, and young children:*

- **Don't** eat shark, swordfish, king mackerel, or tilefish (sometimes called golden bass or golden snapper) because they contain high levels of mercury.

- **Eat** up to 12 ounces (two average meals) a week of a variety of fish and shellfish that are lower in mercury. Shrimp, canned light Tuna, salmon, Pollock, and catfish are low-mercury fish. Albacore ("white") tuna has more mercury than canned light tuna. So limit your intake of albacore tuna to once a week.

**What If You Hate Fish?** *I say you haven't found your fish yet.*

Not all omega-3 fats come from fish. In fact, Americans also consume plant omega-3s in the form of alpha-linolenic acid (ALA), which is found in flax seeds, walnuts, and a few vegetable oils.

Another analysis, from the Health Professionals Follow-up Study, showed that higher intake of ALA may be particularly important for protection against heart disease in people who didn't eat much fish.

# Get Essentials Oils To Be Healthy Eating Seafood.

Seafood contains essential oils that are an important part of your diet. Oils provide the source of energy we need, and they are also great flavor enhancers. More importantly, they are a source of significant fatty acids.

Seafood oils are unique and have great nutritional benefits to our body. This oil contains the omega-3 polyunsaturated fatty acids, specifically the eicosapentaenoic acid (EPA) and docosahexaenoic acid (DHA).

Our body only produces small amounts of these important fatty acids; therefore we need to rely on other sources for this essential nourishment. **Seafood** is one of the best sources of these nutrients. In fact, oils are the second biggest components in most seafood.

*Eating fresh seafood is a great way to obtain your required dose of these essential oils. Oils extracted from seafood are also available as nutritional supplements.*

Oils derived from seafood help prevent some of the most deadly diseases today, including Alzheimer's disease, asthma, arteriosclerosis, bipolar disorder, bronchitis, cancer, heart diseases and more.

*According to recent findings, Omega-3 also helps improve people's immune functions, thereby reducing infections.*

- Seafood oils are known to have properties that lower blood pressure, benefiting especially those suffering from hypertension.

# So many nut butters, so many questions.

We have been attempting to make healthier choices when eating out lately, but found myself dazed as to which of the nut variety spreads found would make the best option.

*Are other nut butters healthier than peanut butter?*

### Peanut Butter

I don't need to tell you that this is it: the king of nut butters. It has about 200 calories per serving (two tablespoons), so don't choke down a whole jar. And it has roughly 16 grams of fat, but it's mostly the good kind -- mono-unsaturated fats. (In fact, peanut butter is equal to olive oil when it comes having a balance of saturated and unsaturated fats.) At roughly 6 carbs and 8 grams of protein, it's ideal for those watching their starch intake and for providing energy. It's also a good source of Vitamins B3 and E, plus minerals such as magnesium.

## So why choose an alternative butter?

### Almond Butter

The almond is classified as a tree nut for culinary purposes, but it's not a nut in the botanical sense. It's the seed of a fruit tree, and it's more closely related to the peach than anything else. This means that some people who are allergic to peanuts (which are legumes) -- but who can tolerate tree nuts like almonds and cashews -- can turn to almond butter as an alternative. (Those allergic to both peanuts and tree nuts can always turn to sunflower seed butter.)

It also has a smooth, mild, naturally sweet flavor and a texture not dissimilar to peanuts when ground and emulsified. These are the main reasons you'll find almond butter so readily available in stores -- much more so than any other peanut butter alternative.

> *While it's true that almond butter is lower in saturated fat than peanut butter, it has a slightly higher fat content overall at roughly 17 to 18 grams per serving. It has the same amount of carbs (6 grams per serving), but packs a lower protein punch than peanut butter at only 5 to 7 grams per serving. Calories are the same, however: 200 calories.*

### *Cashew Butter*

Cashews are also seeds, like almonds. But they're not necessarily a good alternative for those with peanut or tree nut allergies. Cashew allergies aren't as common as peanut allergies, but those allergic to peanuts are often sensitive to cashews as well.

Unfortunately, however, because cashews have such a high starch content, they also make the nut butter with the most carbs per serving (8 to 10) and the least amount of protein (4 to 6 grams) of the trio. On the plus side, cashew butter is lower in fat overall -- despite its oily flavor -- with only 14 to 16 grams per serving (although it doesn't provide any omega-3 fatty acids, as peanut and almond butter do).

> *They're also the lowest in terms of calories, at between 160 and 190 calories per serving. Cashew butter is also high in copper, magnesium and phosphorus, but doesn't pack the vitamin punch that almond butter does.*

## Dietary fats and oils:

There are two types of dietary fats, visible and non-visible fat. *Visible fats* include oils, butter, animal fat etc. *Invisible fat*, not visible to naked eyes, is present in food items like wheat, rice and pulses, etc. in small amounts. In general, the fats and oils we use are mainly composed of either saturated OR unsaturated fatty acid chains.

> *Saturated fats* contain no double bonds in their chemical structure. They exist in a *solid state at room temperatures*, and, usually derived from animal sources, although some of them are obtained from plant sources. Examples: butter, lard, palm kernel oil, coconut oil, etc.

> Unsaturated fats contain one or more double bonds in their chain. They are liquid at room temperatures and in general, derived from plant sources. Examples include soybean oil, safflower oil, etc. Fish oil, however, is composed of a major proportion of unsaturated fats to saturated fats.

## Limitations of fats and oils

Apart from the need for fat-soluble vitamins and essential fatty acids, there is no specific requirement for dietary fats and oils as long as the diet provides adequate nutrients for energy. Excess carbohydrates in the form of glucose ultimately convert into fatty acids under the influence of insulin hormone. Those who consume omega-6 and omega-3 fats at the ratio of more than 10:1 should compensate by consuming omega-3 rich foods like fish, greens and algae.

Excess fats in the diet circulate as *triglycerides* and *cholesterol* in the blood. These components deposit at various proportions in different organs and tissues inside our body leading to obesity, coronary artery disease, diabetes, peripheral vascular disease, stroke.

Current recommendations are to limit dietary fat to **30%** or less of **total calories**. No more than 5-10% of energy should come from saturated fats, 10% should be from mono-unsaturated and another 10% from poly-unsaturated fatty acids.

### *So Many Oils, So Little Time*

Not all oils are created equal. In fact, no one oil can be used for all things; instead, each has its distinct place in the kitchen. Keep these basic categories in mind when you're cooking:

For baking: Coconut, palm, canola and high oleic safflower and sunflower oil work best.

For frying: Because they stand up well to the heat, avocado, peanut, palm and sesame oil are ideal.

For sautéing: Many oils are great for sautéing, including avocado, canola, coconut, grape seed, olive, sesame and high oleic safflower and sunflower oils.

For dipping, dressings and marinades: When it comes to making dressings and marinades, or finding oil that's perfect to serve alongside crusty bread for dipping, you're looking for terrific flavor. For this purpose look to flax, olive, peanut, toasted sesame or walnut oil.

## *Oil 101*

We know there are a lot of oils on our shelves!

- Avocado Oil: Pressed from avocados, this smooth, nutty oil is more than 50% mono-unsaturated, making it a heart-nourishing choice. Use it in salad dressings or to sauté fish, chicken, sweet potatoes or plantains.

- Canola Oil: Canola is actually a cousin to cabbage and Brussels sprouts. In fact, it's a variety of rapeseed that's part of the mustard family, which includes those above-mentioned veggies. It's beneficial for heart health thanks to its fatty acid profile and omega-3 and low saturated fat contents and perfect for light cooking.

- Coconut Oil: Pressed from the fruit of the coconut palm tree, coconut oil is ideal for light fair and subtly flavored dishes. This oil is particularly mouth-watering to use for making popcorn and hash browns.

- Corn Oil: Most corn oil is extracted only from the germ of the corn kernel and is golden yellow in color; unrefined oil will have a darker color and richer corn taste. Use in salad dressings and dips with stronger flavors like peppers or garlic.

- Grape seed Oil: Grape seed oil is extracted from the seeds of grapes, a byproduct of the wine-making industry. Use it on salads and raw veggies or in dips, sauces and salsas.

- Olive Oil: A mainstay of the Mediterranean diet and one of the oldest known culinary oils, olive oil contains predominately **heart-friendly** mono-unsaturated fat. Extra virgin olive oil results from the first cold-pressing of olives while mild "pure" olive oil is a blend of refined olive oil and extra virgin olive oil.

- Peanut Oil: It's relatively high mono-unsaturated content makes it **heart-healthy**. Peanut oil is superior for frying, light sautéing and stir-fries.

- Sesame Oil: The seed of the sesame plant provides sesame oil, which has a high antioxidant content. Unrefined sesame oil is great as a key flavor component in sauces or dressings. Use refined sesame oil for high heat applications like frying and toasted sesame oil for stir fries and Asian sauces and dips.

**To Refine or Not to Refine?**

Some oils are refined to make them more stable and suitable for high temperature cooking. Keep in mind, though, that the process removes most of the flavor, color and nutrients from the oils, too.

On the other hand, unrefined oil is simply pressed and bottled so it retains its original nutrient content, flavor and color. Unrefined oils add full-bodied flavor to dishes and are best used for low- or no-heat applications.

**The Facts on Fats:**

- Fats and oils also play crucial roles in stabilizing blood sugar levels, providing raw materials for making hormones and contributing to a healthy immune system.

Fats also make a large contribution to the taste, aroma and texture of food — those things that give us such satisfaction when dining.

**Triglycerides**

Simply stated, triglycerides are the chemical form of fats in food and in the body. Think of fats as a building and triglycerides as the bricks that give it shape. Every triglyceride "brick" consists of a mixture of three fatty acids — saturated, mono-unsaturated and polyunsaturated (the "tri"), and one glycerol molecule. Thus, the name "tri"-"glyceride."

A particular fat is defined by the combination of fatty acids that make up its "bricks." The triglyceride bricks in olive oil, for example, have many more mono-unsaturated fatty acids than it does saturated or polyunsaturated fatty acids, making olive oil a mono-unsaturated fat.

## **Mono-unsaturated**

- Mono-unsaturated fats are heart-healthy because they maintain good **HDL** cholesterol levels while lowering bad LDL cholesterol levels.

They are more chemically stable than polyunsaturated fat but not as stable as saturated fat. This means they keep better than polyunsaturated oils but not as well as saturated oils. They are most appropriate for light cooking or used raw in salad dressings and the like.

- Oils that are predominantly ***mono-unsaturated*** include olive, avocado, peanut, sesame, lard and duck fat. When stored at room temperature, mono-unsaturated fats are typically liquid, but they are likely to solidify when stored in the refrigerator.

Mono-unsaturated oils are generally considered to be the healthiest overall, but it's important to note that all three types have distinct advantages and disadvantages — not just for health but for flavor and culinary characteristics as well.

## Polyunsaturated

Polyunsaturated fatty acids are more susceptible to rancidity than saturated and mono-unsaturated fatty acids, especially after prolonged contact with oxygen, light or heat. Oils that are predominately polyunsaturated include walnut, grape seed, soy, corn and fish oils. *These are liquid at room temperature.*

## Saturated

Saturated fats are the most chemically stable, giving them a long shelf life and the ability to withstand high cooking temperatures. Typically solid at room temperature, saturated fats are found primarily in *animal fats and tropical oils.*

## Animal Fats

In general, animal fats such as butter, cream and tallow are predominantly saturated, however, two of the most highly saturated fats — *coconut oil and palm kernel oil* — come from vegetable sources.

- Animal fats like lard, chicken fat and duck fat are predominantly mono-unsaturated, while fish oils are predominantly polyunsaturated.

- Fatty acid composition of animal fat can vary depending on the diet of the animal.

Butter is the most common animal fat in the kitchen and good quality butters abound, as do cream and other dairy-based products used in cooking.

**Trans Fats:** *The Very Worst Kind*

- *Trans fatty acids are chemically altered, man-made fats found in partially hydrogenated oils.*

The hydrogenation process, in common use since the early 20th century, injects hydrogen into vegetable fats under high heat and pressure. This saturates what was previously an unsaturated fat and results in a chemical configuration that is not found in nature and is very rich in trans fatty acids. This is done to make vegetable oils, which are normally liquid at room temperature, solid (Crisco) and more chemically stable, thereby extending the shelf life of products in which they are used.

Trans fats are doubly harmful because they *lower* HDL (good) cholesterol and *raise* LDL (bad) cholesterol levels, increasing the risk of coronary heart disease. In fact, trans fatty acids have an even worse impact on cholesterol levels than diets high in butter, which contain saturated fat. A 2002 report by the Institute of Medicine (a branch of the National Academy of Sciences) concluded that trans fats ***are not safe to consume*** in any amount.

# A List of Common Nutritional Terms

**Serving Size:** All serving sizes have been set by the FDA[24]. All of the information below pertains to….

**Calories:** *this amount of food.*

Calories are figured from the amount of fat, carbohydrate, and protein in the food.

---

24   https://www.fda.gov/files/food/published/Food-Labeling-Guide-%28PDF%29.pdf

**Calories from Fat:**

This shows how many calories come from fat. To find the ***Percentage of Calories Derived from Fat***, divide Calories from Fat by total Calories. In this case, this food gets 5 of its 150 calories from fat, or 3%.

**% Daily Value[25]:**

This is a way that you can evaluate how a particular food fits into your daily meal plan. These percentages are based on health agency guidelines listed in the footnote at the bottom of the label, for a person eating 2,000 calories in a day. This food item provides only 1% of the amount of fat that a person eating 2,000 calories would consume in a day. **Daily Values do not indicate the percentage of a nutrient in a food** — for instance, the Daily Value for fat does NOT show the percentage of calories from fat.

**Total Fat:**

Many people are watching how much fat they eat. Total fat consists of four subtypes of fat: saturated fat, trans fat, mono-unsaturated fat, and polyunsaturated fat.

**Saturated Fat:**

This is a fat that's linked with high blood cholesterol. (Saturated fat can be rounded to 0 grams if less than 1/2 gram per serving).

**Trans Fat:**

This is a fat that's linked with high blood cholesterol. (maybe 0 grams if less than 1/2 gram per serving).

---

25   https://www.fda.gov/food/new-nutrition-facts-label/daily-value-new-nutrition-and-supplement-facts-labels

**Cholesterol:**

Cholesterol is only found in products of animal origin. If a product has very little cholesterol (less than 2 mg per \ serving), this value can be rounded down to zero mg.

**Sodium:**

High levels of sodium are found in salt, soy sauce, condiments, processed foods, cured meats and cheese. Some people are very salt sensitive. Others can eat sodium without ill effects. (sodium can be rounded to 0 grams if less than 5 mg per serving).

**Total Carbohydrate:**

Carbohydrates contain three categories: simple carbohydrates (sugars); complex carbohydrates (starches); and dietary fiber.

> Dietary fiber are carbohydrates that aren't digested by human enzymes. They're only found in foods of plant origin, and provide roughage or bulk to our foods.

**Sugars:**

Sugars can be naturally occurring, like the fructose in fruit and juice, or lactose in milk. They can also be from refined sources, such as table sugar (sucrose), corn syrup, or molasses. The FDA has not determined a ***Daily Value*** for sugar. (Sugars can be rounded to 0 grams if less than 1/2 gram per serving).

**Protein:**

Protein is the building material of our bodies. The FDA has determined that most Americans get more than enough protein, and does not require a daily value listing.

**Vitamins and Minerals:**

These numbers list the percentage of the USRDA of these nutrients. USRDA stands for *United States Recommended Daily Allowance.*

**Percent Daily Values Footnote:**

Health agencies, such as the American Heart Association, have set guidelines for healthy eating. This footnote sets out guidelines that apply to people eating 2,000 or 2,500 calories. These guidelines don't change from label to label. **They do not represent what's in the food you're buying.** Instead, these numbers are used to calculate the Daily Values column above.

**Calories per gram Footnote:**

These numbers are constants. Every *gram of fat has 9 calories.* A gram of carbohydrate or *protein has 4 calories* each. For instance, this food has 0.5 grams of fat. You would multiply 0.5 by 9 to get 4.5, which is rounded up to 5 Calories from Fat.

**Fat Free:**

Product has less than 1/2 (0.5) grams of fat per serving.

**99% Fat Free:**

Every 100 grams of food will have 1 gram or less of fat.

**Low Fat:**

Product has 3 grams of fat or less per serving.

**Light (Lite):**

Product has 33% fewer calories of 50% less fat per serving than a comparable product.

**Lean:**

For meat and poultry only. Product has less than 10 grams fat, less than 4 grams saturated fat, and less than 95 milligrams cholesterol per serving.

**Low Calorie:**

Product has 40 calories or less per serving.

**Saturated Fat Free:**

Product has less than 0.5 grams saturated fat per serving. This value will be rounded to zero.

**Trans Fat Free:**

Product has less than 0.5 grams trans-fat per serving. This value will be rounded to zero.

**Low in Saturated Fat:**

Product has 1 gram or less saturated fat per serving.

**Cholesterol Free:**

Product has less than 2 milligrams of cholesterol per serving. This value will be rounded to zero.

**Low Cholesterol:**

Product has 20 milligrams or less cholesterol and 2 grams or less of saturated fat per serving.

**Sodium Free:**

Product has less than 5 milligrams of sodium per serving. This value will be rounded to zero.

**Very Low Sodium:**

Product has 35 milligrams or less of sodium per serving.

**Low Sodium:**

Product has 140 milligrams or less of sodium per serving.

**Good Source:**

Used for fiber, protein, vitamins, or minerals. Product has at least 10% of the Daily Value for that particular nutrient.

**High in (Excellent Source):**

Used for fiber, protein, vitamins or minerals. Product has at least 20% of the Daily Value for the particular nutrient.

# Background Recipes:

## The Gluten Free Flour ~*alternative recipes*

**Ingredients:**

| | |
|---|---|
| 160 grams | Brown rice flour, superfine |
| 160 grams | White rice flour, superfine |
| 80 grams | Tapioca starch |
| 80 grams | Potato starch |
| 20 grams | Potato flour |
| 18 grams | Xanthan gum |
| 8 grams | Pectin, pure powdered |

**Directions:**

Place all ingredients in a large bowl, and whisk to combine well. The pectin should be used without the calcium packet. Store in an airtight container at room temperature until ready to use. The recipe can be halved or used in multiples easily. Just be sure to whisk fully in a large enough container.

## Generic GF flour blend

**Ingredients:**

| | |
|---|---|
| 180 grams | White rice flour, superfine |
| 145 grams | Cornstarch, Gluten-free |

| | |
|---|---|
| 85 grams | Tapioca starch |
| 80 grams | Brown rice flour, superfine |
| 60 grams | Nonfat dry milk, gluten-free |
| 20 grams | Potato starch |
| 10 grams | Xanthan gum |

**Directions:**

In a blender or food processor, grind the nonfat dry milk into a fine powder. Place all ingredients in a large bowl, and whisk to combine well. Store in an airtight container at room temperature until ready to use. The recipe can be halved or used in multiples easily. Just be sure to whisk fully in a large enough container. This recipe makes just over 4 cups.

# GF Cake Flour

Makes 4 1/2 cups.

I can make a cake without special flour blends, but you may find that you want to create a lighter version of a muffin or the like. This cake flour is perfect for that.

**Ingredients:**

520 grams All-purpose gluten-free flour (like coconut)
112 grams Cornstarch

**Directions:**

In a blender or food processor, grind the coconut flour into an "all-purpose" flour texture to eliminate the gritty texture everyone complains about. In a large bowl, whisk the gluten-free flour and cornstarch together. Transfer to an airtight container and store until ready to use.

# A Gum Free GF Flour Blend

This is a great blend for gluten-free pancakes, where xanthan gum really creates issues causing the pancakes to cook too fast.

**Ingredients:**

| | |
|---|---|
| 140 grams | White rice flour |
| 47 grams | Potato starch |
| 23 grams | Tapioca starch or flour |

**Directions:**

Combine all ingredients in a large bowl and whisk together. Store in an airtight container until ready to use. Makes about 1 1/2 cups, plenty for one recipe. Double or triple it if you like to eat pancakes a lot!

# Probiotics

Learn the basics of supplementing your diet with healthy bacteria.

WHAT ARE PROBIOTICS?

Ideally, probiotics are living, cultured bacterial strains ingested in hope that they will cultivate in the intestine and replenish the healthy intestinal flora often depleted as a result of stress, poor diet, sickness, and antibiotics. In carefully selecting individual bacterial strains, like L. Acidophilus and Bifidobacterium bifidum, known for their ability to enhance digestive and immune system function, companies manufacture products that they believe are capable of safely transporting beneficial, live bacteria into the intestine.

HOW DO PROBIOTICS WORK?

Arriving in the intestines, probiotics multiply, forming colonies that attempt to crowd out the many pathogenic bacteria that can be detrimental to overall health. It may be helpful to think of the digestive track as a bacterial "parking lot" with a limited number of "parking spaces." If we consume probiotics and allow enough good bacteria to steal intestinal parking spots, the bad bacteria are forced to keep moving and are eventually driven from the intestine or die off.

WHO SHOULD TAKE PROBIOTICS?

For those seeking products to improve digestive health and strengthen immune response, introducing a probiotic supplement could be the answer. In short, probiotics cater to everyone, with products formulated specifically for infants, children, teens, adults, the elderly and even pets. While certainly not a cure for any disease, you may find that probiotics aid in the maintenance and proper function of your digestive tract and immune system.

## HOW DO I PICK A PROBIOTIC PRODUCT?

With so many competing companies, products, and bacterial strains, the proliferation of information can be difficult to digest! It's important to consider the strains of bacteria used, potency, shipping process, culture methods, delivery system, and price point when choosing a probiotic.

# Index:

## A:

Acknowledgments .... p. 25
Almond Butter...p. 204
Almond crunchies, recipe....p. 113-114
Alternative protein ..... p. 73
Aminos ..... p. 67-70
Ancho-Onion Jam, recipe ....p. 101
Animal vs Plant proteins ....p. 72
Apples, why they are good .... p. 58
Arugula, apple, pineapple, blueberry salad, recipe...p. 120
Asian Spice blend, recipe ..... p.92
Asparagus, peach, tomato salad, recipe...p. 113
Avocado butter, herbed, recipe ..... p. 147
Avocado Oil ....p. 192

## B:

Banana smoothie, recipe .... p 189
Background recipes.... P. 202
Bean cookery .....p .177, 193-194
Beans, Dictionary....p. 194-197
Beans, charred, recipe....p. 174
Beef vs. Plant ..... p.74, 88
Beet and mango relish, recipe .....p. 168
Best Food for You .... p.47
Black Bean Bowl, recipe ..... p. 106-108
Boniato ..... p. 147
Braised Greens, recipe. ....p. 171
Brussel Sprouts and Guarapo, Recipe...p. 165
Brussel Sprout, mango salad, recipe... p 116

## C:

Cancer looks like this ..... p.49
Cancer, what does it feed on ..... p. 49
Cancer, fighting foods .... p. 51
Cantaloupe.... P. 65
Cashew Butter...p. 205
Cauliflower, buffalo style, recipe ..... p. 128
Cauliflower, Dukkah, recipe ..... p.170
Cauliflower, mango, lime, recipe...p. 166
Catechin, flavonoid .... p. 62
Cherimoya .... p. 62
Chia or Flax seeds healthier ..... p. 54-57
Chia Seeds contain ... p. 56-57
Chick Pea pancakes, recipe ..... p. 117
Chickpea Salad...p. 115
Chicken Shawama, recipe ....p .146
Chimi-Churri, recipe ...p. 107
Cholesterol, how to lower .....p 198-200

Coconut Aminos .... p. 67
Coconut, lime, chili seafood marinade ....p. 97
Coconut Syrup, recipe ....p. 112
Corn-Coconut chowder, recipe ..... p. 104
Corn Fritters ..... p. 124
Cruciferous Vegetables ..... p. 58-60
Cucumber wasabi salad, recipe....p. 110
Curcumin, rhizome ....p. 66
Curry Paste, recipe ... p.91
*Curcumin ..... p. 65*

## D:

Dahl, recipe ..... p. 99
Dietary Guidelines ..... p. 11
Dietary Fats and oils .....p.206-7
Dijon, Lime Coconut Aioli, recipe ....p. 96

## E:

Elderberry .... p. 64-65

## F:

Farro, recipe ....134
Fennel salad, pickled, recipe...p. 182-185
Fish, why Important....p. 200-203
Flax seeds ..... p. 51-55
Folate-Rich Foods .... p. 61
Foods that are good for you .... p. 47
Foods that fight for you .... p. 48
Foods to help our Fight .... p. 30, 58
Foreward .... p. 5
Frittata, recipe ..... p. 108
FYI section, recipe ....p.192

## G:

General Tao's Tofu, recipe...p. 102
Ginger ..... p. 67
Gluten-free Cake Flour, recipe ....p. 203
Gluten-free Flour, recipe ....p. 202, 203
Gluten-free Gum-free, Flour, ....p. 204
Gluten-free Meatloaf, recipe ....p. 1159
Gluten-free Pasta, recipe..... p.180
Golden Beet salad, recipe... p. 111
Good for you Healthy Foods ..... p. 42
Grape must p. 153
Graviola, soursop .... p. 61, 62
Greens, braised, recipe...p. 171
Grits, kale, black bean, recipe .....p. 121

## H:

Healing yourself through food .....25
Health Halo, what is a ..... p. 7
Healthy eating ..... p. 6, 19
Healthy proteins ..... p. 46
Healthy Sustainable Diet..... P. 35
High protein foods ..... p. 31
Honey-Mustard dressing, recipe ....p. 103

## I:

Indonesian spice, recipe .... p.91

## K:

Kaizen Cuisine ..... p. 28-32, 82-84
Kale and Quinoa, recipe .....p .123
Kidney Bean .....p .181

## L:

Lycopene .....p. 129
Lentils ..... p .63,
Lentil, red, curry, recipe....p. 175
Lupini Bean....p 181
Longevity research .... p. 19

## M:

Macha Vinaigrette, recipe ..... p.94
Mango Brussel Sprouts salad, recipe...p. 116
Marinara sauce, GF, recipe .... p. 138
Meatloaf, Gluten-free, recipe ....p. 159-162
Meats, why not .... p. 71
Menu Ideas.....p. 39-40
Mediterranean Pasta, recipe ...p.140
Microgreens .... p. 147-9
Mono-saturated fats ..... p. 194
MUFA and PUFA ..... p. 76-79
Mushrooms .... p.75

## N:

Natural Diet .... p. 33-35, 37-39
Nut Butters, Various....p. 204-205
Nutritional Terms.....p. 212-217

## O:

Oils 101 .... p.207-212
Our Journey ...p. 8, 11

## P:

Pad Thai salad, Recipe....p.114
Paleo diet .....p. 18
Pasta, Mediterranean-style, Recipe...p. 145
Pea and lentil Cookery....p. 177
Peach, leek and roasted red Pepper, Recipe...p.109
Pickled Golden Beets, Recipe....p. 112
Pineapple Kimchee .... p.144
Pineapple-Mango spread, recipe.... 103
Pineapple-ranch dressing, recipe...p. 167
Plant based protein..... P. 71, 85
Plant based overview ....p. 85
Plant forward Strategy .... p. 83
Plantain curry stew, recipe...p. 173
Polenta, GF, recipe .... p. 136
Pork, 10 hour, recipe.... P. 152-156
Pork, Asian braised, recipe...p. 141
Protein, alternative ..... p. 74
Protein Flip.... P. 74-76
Personal histories ..... p. 8
Poly-unstaurated Fats .....p. 195
Probotics .....p. 220

## Q:

Quinoa bites, recipes ..... p. 125
Quinoa with Blueberries, recipe ..... p.189
Quinoa superbowl, recipe....p. 149-151

## R:

Recipes ..... p. 90-182, 218-220
Red curry sauce, GF, recipe....p. 177
Resistant Starch....p. 161
Roasted Red Pepper sauce, recipe....p. 96

## S:

Salad Substitution .... p. 39-40
Salad, arugula, pineapple, recipe .... p. 131
Salmon, Asian braised, recipe ..... p. 142
Saturated Fats ..... p.76-79
Scallops,Pan-seared, recipe .... p. 129-133
Seafood, eat to help You.....p. 185-188
Seafood marinade, recipe .... p. 97
Simple menu ideas .... p. 39

Soy , why is it bad for you ..... p. 70, 71
Stir-frys ..... p. 40
Spicy Asian paste, recipe.... P. 93
Sustainable Die ..... p. 35-39
Sweet potato cakes, recipe ..... p. 119
Sweets, recipes ....p. 186

## T:

Tea ....p. 63
Trans-fats ..... p.77, 196
Tobacco flour, recipe ..... p. 152
Tofu, recipe ..... p. 94, 102
Top Cancer fighting Foods....p. 51
Triglycerides ....p. 192
Turkey, Oatmeal and Quinoa meatloaf, recipe ....p. 157-59
Tuscan Kale .....p. 122

## U:

Using this book .... p. 13

## V:

Vegan Bolognese sauce, recipe .....p. 139
Vegan Chocolate pudding, recipe .....p 187
Vegan Onions, recipe .... p. 125, 161
Vegan Pudding, recipe ....p .188
Vegan Potatoes, recipe .... p. 163
Vegan Red Curry sauce ....p .159
Vegan Red Lentil Curry, recipe..... P. 157
Veggie Pot, recipe ..... p. 164
Vitamin D ....p. 62

## W:

Wahoo, recipe ....p. 98
Why read this book....p.5
What Does Cancer Feed on .... p.50

## Y:

Yam and White bean, recipe....p.135

## Z:

Za'atar Spice, recipe .... p.136

## Chef Michael Bennett's other books:

180 pages 100+ recipes

Michael's first book was written with healthy Tropical cooking tendencies touting the recipes used in the Caribbean when he lived for years.
2011
ISBN: 978-0615297781

272 pages 125+ recipes

Michael's first book was rewritten to be Gluten Free in 2011 and became then became "Flavor Quest". All Medi-bbean recipes.
2014
ISBN: 978-1495117619

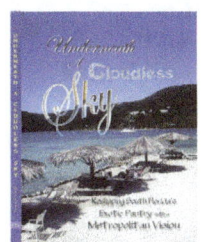

Michael's second book was written with emphasis on a multitude of exotic South Florida grown food. You will find healthy "metropolitan" plate compositions and recipe styling that touts the foods he used in Miami's finest dining venues.
2011
**ISBN: 978-0615328775**

*190 pages 100+ recipes*

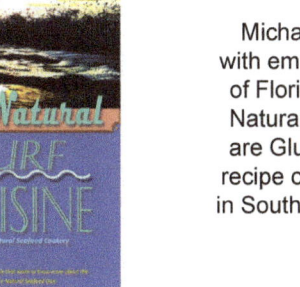

Michael's next cookbook was written with emphasis on an "All-Natural" bounty of Florida's finest seafood. You will find Natural foods presented in recipes that are Gluten Free and heart healthy. The recipe compositions tout menus he used in South Florida's most innovative restaurants. Circa 2014
**ISBN: 9781495105982**

*165 pages 110+ recipes*

Michael's most innovative "Medi-bbean" recipe composition mixes the Mango's importance in our legendary South Florida's - "Tropical ingredients", with the healthy cookery techniques of Mediterranean nations. You will find heart-healthy and Gluten-Free recipes touting menus he used in South Florida's most innovative restaurants. Circa 2017
**ISBN: 978-1532330698**

*212 pages 100+ recipes*

Chef Michael Bennett has cataloged countless culinary expressions and, quips of wisdom, from South Florida's best chefs.
Our (culinary) art form is one of oral and visual training passed down from one generation to another. 2014
**ISBN: 978-1450783002**

*172 pages, 0 recipes*

227

www.ingramcontent.com/pod-product-compliance
Lightning Source LLC
Chambersburg PA
CBHW080731230426
43665CB00020B/2696